STUDIES IN ECONOMICS AND POLITICAL SCIENCE

Volume 9

THE GROWTH OF THE BRITISH ECONOMY 1918–1968

THE GROWTH OF THE BRITISH ECONOMY 1918–1968

G. A. PHILLIPS AND R. T. MADDOCK

Routledge
Taylor & Francis Group
LONDON AND NEW YORK

First published in 1973 by George Allen & Unwin Ltd

This edition first published in 2022
by Routledge

4 Park Square, Milton Park, Abingdon, Oxon OX14 4RN

and by Routledge
605 Third Avenue, New York, NY 10017

Routledge is an imprint of the Taylor & Francis Group, an informa business

British Library Cataloguing in Publication Data
A catalogue record for this book is available from the British Library

ISBN: 978-1-03-212459-9 (Set)
ISBN: 978-1-00-322951-3 (Set) (ebk)
ISBN: 978-1-03-212960-0 (Volume 9) (hbk)
ISBN: 978-1-03-212965-5 (Volume 9) (pbk)
ISBN: 978-1-00-322705-2 (Volume 9) (ebk)

DOI: 10.4324/9781003227052

Publisher's Note
The publisher has gone to great lengths to ensure the quality of this reprint but points out that some imperfections in the original copies may be apparent.

Disclaimer
The publisher has made every effort to trace copyright holders and would welcome correspondence from those they have been unable to trace.

The Growth of the British Economy 1918–1968

BY

G. A. PHILLIPS
University of Lancaster

AND

R. T. MADDOCK
University College of Wales, Aberystwyth

London

GEORGE ALLEN & UNWIN LTD

RUSKIN HOUSE MUSEUM STREET

First published in 1973

ISBN 0 04 330233 5 hardback
0 04 330234 3 paperback

Printed in Great Britain
in 10pt Times Roman type
by Alden & Mowbray Ltd
at the Alden Press, Oxford

PREFACE

Throughout the history of industrial societies, economists have been concerned with the nature and causes of economic growth. The purpose of this book is, briefly, to relate this thinking, or some aspects of it, to the historical experience of Britain since the end of the First World War. Our object has been, not to produce any substantial amount of new factual material, but to attempt to leaven known facts with a larger theoretical ingredient.

Our starting point has been the prediction, put forward by the founders of the discipline and repeated for more than a century thereafter, that mature economic systems would inevitably face stagnation. By the end of the First World War empirical evidence seemed partly to have validated this belief so far as the British economy was concerned. Thereafter, of course, the pattern of economic development has come to seem much more complex and resistant to simple generalization. Yet Britain has remained, on the whole, a slow-growing economy during this period, both in relation to her past achievements, and often in comparison with foreign competitors. Much of our attention is thus necessarily focused on the possible reasons for this modest rate of expansion.

We look for such reasons in three main areas. Firstly, we examine the adequacy of the indigenous factors of production and domestic demand (Chapters 2–4). Secondly, we look at international conditions and the effect they had upon Britain through the mechanism of trade and monetary transactions (Chapters 6–7). Thirdly, we examine the main decision-makers in the economic process, and consider some of their policy preferences (Chapters 5 and 8).

As our final chapter acknowledges, the outcome of this discussion is inconclusive. No one factor, nor even any consistent combination of factors, seems adequately to account for the course of twentieth-century economic development in Britain. If we have given rather more emphasis to international and commercial influences than to others, this probably reflects the currently fashionable diagnosis and a wish not to be tediously non-committal. But any such explanatory preference is hazardous, if only because statistical data on some aspects of the history of this period are clearly inadequate (on the distribution of income, for example); and because certain historical problems (for instance, the role of management in promoting growth) are almost untouched by research.

Authors mentioned in the text and quoted directly and the sources of statistical tables are cited in footnotes; other principal works used and recommended for further reading are listed at the end of each chapter. Throughout the references the place of publication of books is London, unless otherwise stated.

We should like to thank the editor, Mr Charles Carter, for his suggestions and corrections, and Professor Graham Rees for reading the chapter on the balance of payments. Robert Bacon and George Bain kindly lent us some statistics which they had been collecting for publication. We are also grateful to Mrs Mary Jones for typing the whole of our main draft.

R.T.M.
G.A.P.

CONTENTS

CHAPTER 1

The Pattern of Growth in the Twentieth Century

In their analyses of economic systems, economists and economic historians have been concerned to discover 'laws' of economic behaviour. Although the main emphasis of 'modern' economics has been on static problems, for instance the determination of prices under various market organizations or of the distribution of the national product, much attention has been directed to the dynamic problems of economic development in industrial societies.

This dynamic analysis has been concerned not just with the basic cause of economic growth, but also with the historical *pattern* of growth. Is there an inevitable tendency for the secular rate of economic growth in industrial societies to slow down as they reach maturity, to suffer what the classical economists called the onset of the Stationary State?[1] Even where economists have agreed that such a tendency to retardation exists, its origins and precise nature have often been in dispute. For some the inherent cause is in the limited productivity of the land, for others it is part of the exploitatory, and hence contradictory nature of the capitalist system, while yet others see the very success of the capitalist system as heralding its demise.[2] Some see the slowing down as part of a continuous evolutionary process, while others see it as the outcome of a series of worsening crises in the system.[3]

Ricardo, who introduces the themes of much of this economic theorizing, also sets a distinct tone to the discussion of economic retardation. The key to economic expansion is the accumulation of capital, which is not immediately consumed but is reinvested in the economic system and adds to its reproductive capacity. Capital accumulation is financed from profits, and remains high so long as they do. But if profits are squeezed the possibility of providing the

[1] E.g. J. S. Mill *Principles of Political Economy* Ed. J. Ashley (1929), book IV, chap. V.

[2] D. Ricardo *Principles of Political Economy and Taxation* Ed. P. Sraffa; K. Marx *Capital* (Moscow 1961); J. Schumpeter *The Theory of Economic Development* (Cambridge, Mass. 1934).

[3] Mill, op. cit.; Marx, op. cit.

requisite amount of capital for growth is correspondingly reduced. Unfortunately, there is, according to Ricardo, an inherent tendency for profits to fall in the long run which will in turn reduce capital accumulation and hence economic growth.

Despite periodic disclaimers to the contrary, Ricardo accepted as a basis for economic analysis the labour theory of value;[4] that is, the value of a commodity is determined by the quantity of labour embodied in its production. It is thus quite possible, for instance, for wages to rise or fall without there being a change in 'value' and hence without there being a change in price (which is simply a representation of value). Wages are usually forced to subsistence levels due to Malthusian population pressures. Apart from certain cultural requirements the level of subsistence is mainly determined by the price of wheat, the basic foodstuff. However, due to the niggardliness of nature, land is of uneven quality. Obviously the most fertile tracts of land will be worked first, providing food at a low cost. As the population increases, less fertile land will have to be brought into cultivation, thus raising the cost of producing wheat on these now marginal units. Since only one price can prevail in the market the price of all wheat (assuming the same quality) is raised to the cost of producing at the marginal (least fertile) plot of land. Owners of intra-marginal land will obtain a rent which is equal to the difference between the market price and their (lower) cost of growing the wheat. Because of the importance of wheat in the diet of the mass of the members of society, the increase in the price of wheat will lead to an increase in the cost of living. Workers will be forced to compensate for this by seeking an increase in wages. However, the manufacturer cannot then automatically push up prices to offset the wage increase. Profits, the difference between cost of production (mainly wages) and price, are gradually pared. So is set up a long-term tendency towards a decline in the level of profits in capitalist economies. It may be possible to postpone this development, notably by technical change which would enhance the productivity of capital, although classical economists as a whole tended to underestimate the importance of innovation in the growth process. Ricardo also puts great emphasis on the ending of the corn laws which would reduce prices at a stroke. But such developments only delay the onset of the Stationary State. The falling rate of profit will gradually reduce the incentive to accumulate capital, which alone provides growth, so that finally it will induce only the bare level of investment sufficient to renew the capital stock worn out

[4] Ricardo, op. cit., chap. I, section I.

by the normal process of production, at which point the economy would stop producing.

Ricardo viewed the onset of the Stationary State with grim foreboding, for its attainment would inevitably set up conflict between the various classes of society. Wages would be maintained at their subsistence level, profits would be squeezed to a minimum, but rents accruing to landlords would rise correspondingly. Most economists of the next generation accepted his arguments, though not all were affected with the same sense of gloom. J. S. Mill, for instance, regarded the Stationary State as one in which members of society would accept their position in the economic order, and devote themselves to the more enhancing pursuit of the arts and general culture.[5]

Though Marx, too, is obviously concerned with the decline of capitalist economies, he fixes more attention than does Ricardo on the subject of economic growth. His debt to the tradition of classical economics is evident, however, in that the central concept of his account of industrial expansion is the Labour Theory of Value.[6] Labour, the source of value, possesses one crucial characteristic: it can produce, in value terms, more than is required to maintain itself at subsistence.

While labour is the source of value it requires the assistance of other factors of production to enable it to create this value. Total value can be said to be composed of three elements:

c. is fixed capital and is made up of the capital equipment and machinery necessary for production
v. is the value of labour power
s. is the surplus value created by labour and referred to above.

Because of the peculiar nature of the system, the capitalist is able to exploit the workers, i.e. to expropriate for his own benefit that which rightfully belongs to the workers. This rate of exploitation is measured as s/v. The rate of profit by which the capitalist measures his achievement is primarily determined by the exploitation function, though it depends also on the amount of capital expenditure. It is given by the ratio $s/v+c$.

The capitalist is always concerned to increase the amount of surplus value he can expropriate from the workers. This is achieved through capital accumulation allied to technical progress. Technical progress by increasing the efficiency of labour will (so long as wages

[5] Mill, op. cit., book IV, chap. VI.
[6] Marx, op. cit., p. 38.

remain at subsistence level) automatically increase the surplus value produced by labour power. However, the very act of capital formation induces a fall in the rate of profit. For by increasing capital at the expense of labour the organic composition of production is changed, i.e. the ratio $c/c+v$ is increased. If capital grows faster than the factor of labour power, however, the ratio of fixed costs to surplus value must also diminish. In other words the rate of profit $s/c+v$ declines, even whilst total profits continue to increase. Even though the capitalist is aware that as he instals new (and better) capital equipment the profit rate is reduced, he is forced to do so by the competitive nature of the system. Thus the changing organic composition of the productive system induces a long-term fall in the level of profits which has the effect of debilitating the system.

Into his theory of industrial development Marx incorporates a theory of economic crises.[7] There may be a variety of causes for a crisis, e.g. a temporary rise in wages which reduces the rate of profit and the rate of growth. However, the most important cause is that of underconsumption. The effect of introducing new machinery incorporating modern techniques of production is to increase the technical efficiency of the productive system. On the other hand the increasing concentration of productive power and Malthusian population pressures enlarge the proletariat, ensure that wages are kept down, and provide the Industrial Reserve Army of unemployed. The ability of the proletariat to consume is reduced and is not offset by increasing consumption by the capitalist; mass consumption falls behind mass production. There emerges a contradiction between the technical and social organization of the economic system. Periodic slumps accentuate the secular trend of falling profit, making the entire economic system unstable. As the capitalist economy matures, the inherent contradictions are magnified, the crises become more frequent and more intense and recovery therefrom weaker, until eventually the entire capitalist system is overthrown.

Even as Marx was writing, however, the classical basis of his analysis was undermined by the advent of the neo-classical marginal analysis of the 1870s. Although this was a great contribution to economic understanding, the logic of the analysis led to an undue concentration on static analysis. On the whole, despite occasional signs of concern with the possibility of stagnation,[8] the marginalists' contribution to an understanding of economic growth was not very

[7] Marx, op. cit., vol. III, part III, chap. XV; K. Marx *Theories of Surplus Value* (1969), part II, chap. XVII.

[8] K. Wicksell *Lectures on Political Economy* (1934), vol. I, part III, p. 209.

substantial. The subsequent dominance of the school led to shift of emphasis away from a consideration of dynamic economic problems, and only since World War II has economic growth regained the centre of the stage again. One result is that those economists who continued to work with the problems of economic growth did so outside the mainstream of orthodox economic theory.

One of the greatest of these individualists was undoubtedly the Austrian economist Joseph Schumpeter. In the neo-classical system the entrepreneur or decision-maker was regarded as an autonomous factor perfectly divisible and in completely elastic supply, who thus could be ignored from the point of view of economic analysis. For Schumpeter, however, the entrepreneur was the key to economic development and growth.[9] He united the static general equilibrium analysis of the neo-classical economists with the dynamic and historical growth theory of Marx. At the very centre of the entire system was the innovating entrepreneur, who far from being the mere manager of a plant was the catalyst by which old forms of economic organization were replaced by new and more efficient forms. In this respect the entrepreneurs were revolutionaries, for they not only changed the methods of production but by so doing widened the vision of what was possible within the economic system. They were 'creatively destructive', for in building a new economic structure they destroyed the old. For a variety of economic and sociological reasons such innovators tended to appear in large numbers at particular periods of time. Their simultaneous emergence transformed economic society, which for a long time would work out and hence benefit from the economic and technical possibilities created by their initial innovations. In this secondary period, however, growth would be lower than in the comparatively short period of frenetic activity which characterized their advent. After the passage of time circumstances might again be propitious for the emergence of another group of entrepreneurs who through their creative/destructive activities would once again push the system along the road of economic development. Thus economic societies would progress by bursts of economic activity followed by periods of comparatively slow growth. In economic terms, the system was self-perpetuating and showed no secular trend towards a Stationary State of low growth. However, speaking as social prophet rather than orthodox economist, Schumpeter suggested that the sheer success of the capitalist system would eventually lead to the end of its dynamic nature. As the economy matures, the size of the average

[9] Schumpeter, op. cit., chap. 2.

production/commercial/economic unit tends to increase. Single individuals find it more difficult to exercise control over such units, and the control of economic resources becomes increasingly concentrated in the hands of organized committees. Decision-making, that most dynamic of activities, becomes more and more a corporate process and *ipso facto* loses its dynamic nature.[10] The corporate attitude is essentially conservative in nature, the possibility of dynamic change is lessened and the economy settles down as it were to a maturity of slow growth.

The sheer success of the Western capitalist system throughout the nineteenth and early twentieth centuries made such writers as forecasted economic doom appear Jeremiahs. But the real possibility of a breakdown in the capitalist system in the inter-war period resulted in a reassessment of the nature of secular decline. In the U.S.A. in particular this was believed by some to be a real possibility, informing the work of the so-called Stagnationists, whose main exponent was Alvin Hansen. One of the causes of a decline in economic growth for the neo-classical economists was the possibility of a too-rapid increase in population.[11] For Hansen the opposite was the case. High growth of population, as for instance in the nineteenth century, promoted economic expansion.[12] If the stimulus of high demographic growth was to disappear and not be replaced by anything else, then expansion would come to an end. Broadly speaking, economic resources could be allocated to either investment or consumption purposes. If population growth were to slow down, the gap between potential output at full employment and actual aggregate consumption demand would grow increasingly large, and unless taken up for investment purposes would inevitably result in unemployed resources.

Investment was determined by a number of factors, the most important by far being the prospective profit rate. Hansen claimed that throughout the nineteenth century, investment had been of the capital widening as opposed to the capital deepening type; thus, even though the proportion of capital to labour had increased there had not been much change in the ratio of capital to output. Profitable investment was limited by the growth in output, which in turn was related to the increase in population. Thus if population growth fell significantly so would investment growth, and in the 1930s this appeared to be a very real prospect.

[10] J. Schumpeter *Capitalism, Socialism and Democracy* (1943), part II.
[11] Wicksell, op. cit., vol. I, chap. III.
[12] A. Hansen *Fiscal Policy* (New York 1941), chap. XVII.

Although it is not a central concern of post-classical economic theory, therefore, the possibility of a secular decline in economic growth has been a fairly constant feature of economic analysis. And as the 'scientific' nature of the subject was emphasized so economists began to make statistical inquiries as to whether there was any empirical evidence of a long-term retardation in industrial societies. Since by the opening of our period Britain was by far the most mature of the industrial economies, the early studies concentrated on the British experience.

Probably the most significant of these early studies was that of the German economist W. Hoffman.[13] According to him, individual industries show a definite pattern of high growth followed by stagnation and decline. However, as old industries decline they are replaced by new ones at their high growth stage. But while growth rates in different industries do vary, Hoffman was in no doubt that the aggregate output of all industries together did follow a sequence of gradually decreasing growth. At least since the late nineteenth century, 'the output of British industries, taken together, has been in the phase of a declining growth of output'.[14] This, moreover, he holds to be an inherent, not an accidental, tendency. He suggests four possible grounds for this conclusion:

(a) The falling rate of population growth. If Ireland is excluded the statistics do show a certain similarity between changes of population growth and of industrial output. Though he does not explain why, Hoffman believes there to be a causal relationship.

(b) Changes in commercial policy, in particular Free Trade, which he believes to have hastened the decline of some inefficient firms.

(c) International developments abroad. These had served to reduce British exports, and thus growth in general. In particular the emergence of Germany and the U.S.A. as important industrial exporting countries meant that Britain had lost some of her traditional overseas markets.

(d) The scarcity of natural resources. Some of Britain's raw materials, coal, iron, copper, etc., had become increasingly more difficult and expensive to obtain, which increased Britain's uncompetitiveness *vis-à-vis* the rest of the world.

For these reasons Hoffman believed that Britain, like other industrial countries, was reaching the stage of economic retardation.

[13] W. Hoffman *British Industry 1700–1950*, trans. W. O. Henderson and H. W. Chaloner (Oxford 1955).

[14] Hoffman, op. cit., p. 206.

His opinion was echoed moreover by other economists working on empirical evidence of growth.[15]

How firmly were such judgements based? Certainly there was statistical evidence of a slowing down in the rate of economic growth by the end of the nineteenth century.[16] But does the British experience after 1919 give any support for this thesis of a general retardation in mature economies?

Possibly the most reliable estimates of growth in the nineteenth and early twentieth centuries are those presented by Deane and Cole. Due to the inadequacy of the data, they warn against putting too much emphasis on particular turning points in the growth rate, and to offset this they present decade averages over thirty-year periods. The figures thus presented do appear to show an unmistakable declining trend in growth.

TABLE 1

Annual Rates of Growth Per Head (Decade Averages Measured over Thirty-Year Period)[17]

	%
1855–64 – 1885–94	2·0
1875–84 – 1905–14	1·5
1890–9 – 1920–9	0·3
1900–9 – 1930–9	0·5

A more detailed set of figures is given by Coppock which once again shows a decisive fall in the growth rate of industrial production up to the outbreak of the First World War.

TABLE 2

Intercyclical Average Annual Growth Rates[18]

	Industrial Production (excluding building)	Productivity
1847–53 – 1854–60	3·5	2·4
1854–60 – 1861–5	1·7	0·6
1861–5 – 1866–74	3·6	2·4
1866–74 – 1875–83	2·1	0·9
1878–83 – 1884–9	1·6	0·2
1884–9 – 1890–9	1·8	0·4
1890–9 – 1900–7	1·8	0·2
1900–7 – 1908–13	1·5	−0·2

[15] W. A. Lewis *Economic Survey 1919–1939* (1949), p. 183.

[16] A. L. Levine *Industrial Retardation in Britain, 1880–1914* (1967).

[17] P. Deane and W. A. Cole *British Economic Growth 1688–1959* (Cambridge 1962), p. 284.

[18] D. J. Coppock, 'The Climacteric of the 1890s, A Critical Note', (*Manchester School of Economic and Social Studies*, vol. 24, 1956).

While the use of long period averages is perfectly justified for the nineteenth century, however, it does have the effect of hiding changes within any one such period. If these changes are of a short term or cyclical nature this might be all to the good. If, however, there appear certain changes which are of long-term significance, the long period average figures may fail to show up these changes till much later. Such appears to be the case here. The Deane and Cole figures show growth declining right up to the outbreak of the Great Depression, whereas there is some evidence that economic growth showed signs of recovery during the 1920s; certainly by the 1930s there is incontrovertible evidence of a strong resurgence in economic growth. There is much current debate as to precisely when the upturn occurred. Given the imprecise nature of much of the information and the condition of economic dislocation which prevailed after 1914, the precise year(s) of the upturn may well be impossible to identify (and is not of great relevance to us here). What is true, however, is that growth was accelerating by the 1930s and may well have been doing so for much of the previous decade as well. Figures for both industrial production and productivity bear this out. Lomax for instance has estimated that for the entire period 1920–37 industrial production increased at an annual average rate of 3·1 per cent which compares with a rate of 1·6 per cent in 1900–13 and 4·6 per cent since the end of the Second World War, and which was approximately the rate of expansion experienced in the great growth period of the nineteenth century, from 1811–60.[19]

Deane and Cole also provide figures for growth of industrial production which show a definite and substantial resurgence in this period. Meanwhile productivity growth also began to increase as the following figures indicate.

TABLE 3

The Rate of Growth of U.K. Industrial Production[a]

(% increases per decade)	%
1860–9 – 1870–9	33·2
1870–9 – 1880–9	20·8
1880–9 – 1890–9	17·4
1890–9 – 1900–9	17·9
1900–9 – 1910–19	12·2
1910–19 – 1920–9	14·1
1920–9 – 1930–8	25·8

[a] Deane and Cole, op. cit., p. 297.

[19] K. Lomax, 'Production and Productivity Movements in the United Kingdom since 1900', *Journal of the Royal Statistical Society*, series A, vol. 122, p. 200.

TABLE 4

Average Rate of Productivity Increase in the U.K.[a]

	%
1870–80	1·39
1880–90	0·59
1890–1900	0·18
1900–14	−0·24
1920–30	3·6
1930–8	1·9
1950–60	2·2

[a] D. Aldcroft and H. Richardson *The British Economy 1870–1939* (1969), p. 225.

Thus despite the vast social and economic problems of unemployment there seems little doubt that 'the inter-war years emerge as a period of growth almost as rapid as any of comparable length in British measured history (post 1865)'.[20] And this rapid growth has occurred right up to the end of the period. The British experience since 1914 thus provides no support at all for the thesis of an inevitable decline of growth as countries reach economic maturity.

Rapid growth was associated with a significant change in the economic and industrial structure of the British economy. The most important aspect of this development was the further enlargement of the manufacturing sector (including gas, electricity and building): its share of G.N.P. rose from 34½ per cent in 1924 to 44½ per cent in 1959. This expansion was clearly connected with the altered constitution of manufacturing; since the beginning of the century the fastest growing industries have been vehicle manufactures, utilities, chemicals and the metal manufacturing group. Agriculture accounted for only 4·2 per cent of G.N.P. in 1924, a proportion which has been more or less maintained up to the present time.

The rapid growth of the G.N.P. in the twentieth century appears to have occurred despite the declining importance of international trade. In 1913 exports accounted for 23 per cent of G.N.P., whereas by 1968 they accounted for 16 per cent. But these figures hide two quite different trends over the period. International trade had traditionally been an important strategic sector in the eighteenth and nineteenth centuries. By the 1920s, however, for a variety of reasons, it had lost its dynamic nature, and gradually became less and less

[20] J. A. Dowie, 'Growth in the Inter-war Period: Some More Arithmetic', *Economic History Review*, April 1968, p. 100.

TABLE 5

% Distribution of the G.N.P. of the U.K.[a]

	1924	1935	1949	1955
Agriculture	4·2	3·9	6·2	4·7
Mines	5·4	3·1	3·7	3·4
Engineering and vehicles	4·7	6·0	11·0	13·4
Metal man	3·3	3·4	5·1	5·4
Textiles	5·2	3·5	4·2	3·3
Clothing	2·5	2·1	1·8	1·5
Food	6·7	5·1	3·5	3·7
Paper	2·3	2·6	2·3	2·7
Chemicals	1·9	2·1	2·2	2·9
Other man	3·2	3·5	3·6	3·7
Gas	1·7	2·5	2·0	2·4
Building	3·1	4·1	5·5	5·7
Rents	6·4	6·5	2·7	3·2
Commerce	17·8	19·6	16·5	15·7
Transport	12·0	10·7	8·2	8·2
Government	4·6	4·7	9·1	9·3
Domestic service	3·4	3·4	0·9	0·6
Income from abroad	5·2	4·1	1·4	1·0

[a] Deane and Cole, op. cit., p. 178.

important. This trend was very much emphasized in the 1930s with the breakdown of the international economy, such that by 1938 exports accounted for only 10 per cent of the G.N.P. After the Second World War, exports again began to grow very rapidly, faster in fact than the growth of G.N.P., and by the end of the period much of the loss of the inter-war period had been made up, with the result that international trade once again plays a vital role in the growth of the economy.

Finally we should notice that a corollary of growth of output has been a different pattern of national income distribution. As the accompanying table shows, since 1900 wages and salaries have

TABLE 6

Distribution of U.K. National Income[a]

	Wages and salaries %	Rents %	Profit, interest and mixed income %
1900–9	48·4	11·4	40·2
1920–9	59·7	6·6	33·7
1930–9	62·0	8·7	29·2
1940–9	68·8	4·9	26·3
1950–9	72·4	4·9	22·7

[a] Deane and Cole, op. cit., p. 247.

increased their share at the expense of both the other principal recipients.

Even though we have established the main outlines of the British experience since the end of the First World War, it might be instructive to compare the British growth record with that of her main rivals; those countries in a roughly similar stage of economic development. Whilst the precise measurement of international growth rates remains difficult, it does appear that over the entire inter-war period the average growth rate of most advanced countries was roughly similar, but that there were significant differences as between the two decades. Average growth for the entire period is given below:

TABLE 7

Growth of G.D.P. 1913–38[a]

	%
Denmark	1·9
France	0·4
Germany	1·6
Italy	1·7
Norway	2·9
Sweden	1·8
U.K.	1·1
U.S.A.	2·0

[a] A. Maddison, 'How Fast Can Britain Grow', *Lloyds Bank Review*, January 1966, p. 3.

Although the evidence is far from conclusive (depending on which index and what base year is chosen), it does appear that in Britain the growth rate of the decade of the thirties was higher than that of the twenties, largely because of the relative stagnation of her old staple industries in the earlier decade. Britain failed to share fully in the general world prosperity of the 1920s. On the other hand when the international economy initially collapsed in the 1930s, trade loses its strategic importance. During this decade Britain's growth is essentially domestically based and the structural change associated with the belated growth of the so-called 'new industries' gives the economy a dynamism lacking in some of the other mature industrial economies. During the 1920s growth of industrial production in Britain averaged 3 per cent per annum compared with 3·7 per cent for the thirties. This compares with a growth rate of 5·5 per cent for Western Europe as a whole in the 1920s and 2 per cent in 1929–38. Annual growth rate of Britain's net national income shows a similarly accelerating trend, increasing from 1·5 per cent in 1920–9 to 2·4 per cent in 1930–9. This increase occurred despite the fact that most estimates of productivity movements (see e.g. Table 4) show a decline over the long period.

Since the Second World War, however, international comparisons have once again been to Britain's disadvantage, as Table 8 makes evident.

TABLE 8

Annual Rate of Growth of Total Output[a]

	1950–60	1960–70
Belgium	2·9	4·7
Denmark	3·3	4·7
France	4·4	5·6
Germany	7·6	4·7
Italy	5·9	5·7
Netherlands	4·9	5·1
Norway	3·5	4·7
Sweden	3·3	4·5
Switzerland	5·1	4·2
U.K.	2·6	2·7
U.S.A.	3·2	4·2
Average	4·2	4·8

[a] A. Maddison *Economic Growth in the West* (1964), p. 28; Organization for European Economic Development *The Outlook for Economic Growth* (Paris 1970).

A similar tale can be seen in comparing productivity figures.[21]

TABLE 9

Annual Average Growth of Output Per Man

	(1) 1950–60	(2) 1960–70
Belgium	2·5	4·2
France	3·9	5·4
Germany	6·0	5·9
Italy	4·1	5·8
Netherlands	3·7	4·9
Norway	3·9	3·7
Sweden	3·5	3·6
U.K.	2·0	3·2
U.S.A.	2·4	2·5
Average	3·5	4·8

[21] Figures obtained from U.N. Economic Survey of Europe (N.Y.) for various years. For comparability some adjustment of the raw figures have been made.

On most indices of economic growth Britain appears towards the bottom of the growth league. Thus even though by historical standards growth in post-war Britain has been very high, there is a general belief that in this period the British economic performance has been bad. How far is this conclusion justified?

The standard of comparison normally taken is that group of countries which have reached a roughly similar stage of economic development, in particular the high growth countries of Western Europe. Compared with this group of countries the British experience has undoubtedly been dissatisfying. It should be pointed out, however, that the differences in the growth rates of Britain and her main competitors vary according to which year is chosen as the base year. Taking 1950 as the base would tend to exaggerate the difference while another base, for instance 1938, reduces this difference and gives more respectability to the British figures.[22]

It has been suggested, more radically, that international comparisons of economic growth are inherently invalid and that the only meaningful comparison to be made is that of the actual growth rate in any one country with that country's productive potential. Productive potential can be defined as the 'output the economy [can] produce under conditions of full employment'.[23] This definition assumes as given the parameters of the economic system, such as the level of technical skill and education, the average level of productivity and the state of the arts. It is thus a short- or medium-term supply concept, but an important one in that the level of resource utilization in one period will obviously influence the productive potential of the succeeding period. To estimate the productive potential a 'normal level' of unemployment is assumed. What is normal is of course impossible to define precisely and depends on what is socially acceptable and on the attainability of economic policy and control objectives. In post-war Britain 'normal' unemployment can be taken to be about 1 to 1½ per cent of the labour force. The productive potential of the economy would thus be the G.N.P. which would have been attained if the economy were constantly operating at an unemployment rate of say 1½ per cent.

However, it would not be possible to obtain the true productive

[22] See J. Knapp and K. Lomax, 'Britain's Growth Performance: The Enigma of the 1950s', *Lloyds Bank Review*, October 1964. This is not to say, of course, that 1938 is in any way a 'better' base than 1950, but simply to point out one of the obvious difficulties of making international comparisons.

[23] A. Okun, 'Potential G.N.P. Its Measurement and Significance', *Proceedings of the American Statistical Association Business and Economic Section*, 1962.

potential merely by multiplying the difference between the actual level of unemployment and the normal by the existing average level of productivity. A change in the level of employment has been shown to affect such variables as hours worked, participation rates in the labour force and, possibly most important of all, the average level of productivity itself.

On the basis of the long-term growth potential of the British economy it has been argued that in fact the British rate of growth, especially in the post-World War II period, has been highly satisfactory. For whilst some countries are inherently fast-growing others are inherently slow-growing, and Britain now falls into the latter category. Though this may be true, however, it may still be instructive to ask why it is that Britain's growth potential is lower than that of most European countries.

High growth is often a concomitant of rapid change in economic structure. Thus the economy with the greater potential for change is likely, other things equal, to experience a high rate of growth. In the inter-war period, certainly in the thirties, Britain enjoyed such an advantage as the economy adapted itself to the establishment of the so-called 'new industries', which gave a boost denied to some other countries. In the post-war period the reverse is true. In particular in Britain the agricultural sector was far less important than in most other countries, and the scope for diverting resources thence to more profitable uses was relatively restricted.

TABLE 10

Relative Share of Primary Sector (Agriculture and Mining) in the Economy 1962–3[a]

	%
Italy	27·8
France	21·1
Denmark	19·1
W. Germany	14·3
Netherlands	12·0
Belgium	9·4
U.K.	6·7

[a] N. Kaldor *Causes of the Slow Rate of Economic Growth of the United Kingdom* (1966).

This point can indeed be generalized: in 1945 the economies of most European countries, due possibly to dislocation caused by two world wars and a violent depression, were less mature than that of

Britain. They were characterized by a large agricultural sector, a lower population density and a low average level of productivity. Some of the post-war experience may be simply a catching-up process as these countries reaped the economic benefit of reconstruction.

If these temporary factors are important, then as they work themselves out the difference in growth potential between Britain and the rest of Western Europe should narrow. In fact, although other prosperous nations, especially Germany, have certainly lost some of the supposed benefits of 'immaturity', there is no real evidence of a general decline in growth in Western Europe. The impression is strengthened that the gap between Britain and Europe will only be narrowed if the growth rate in Britain is increased.

By the middle of the twentieth century early fears regarding the onset of secular stagnation in Britain, and elsewhere in the developed world, had proved to be unfounded. Industrialized countries appeared to be established on a path of self-sustaining growth with every prospect of increased living standards for the majority of people.

However, the growth debate continued; indeed it increased in urgency and stridency. The ground was shifted from a technical discussion of what caused growth and why some countries grew faster or slower than others to the more fundamental, philosophical question of whether further growth was necessary or even justified. The arguments put forward for continued growth were very powerful and long established: the increase in general living standards and in particular the possibility of transferring resources to the poorer sections of the world community. Socialist thinkers saw in growth the prospect of developing the public sector to better serve the community.[24]

On the other hand, the opposing view, which had been limited to a number of radical economists and social thinkers, was taken up by an increasing number of economists who put the argument in strictly economic terms.

Basic to the idea that economic growth is desirable is the belief that the free market system correctly allocates economic resources to meet human wants. Thus, if individual preferences operating with the price system indicate that resources should be allocated in such a way that growth is maintained, then, with certain obvious exceptions, resources are optimally allocated. It is this view that has been increasingly challenged.

[24] C. A. R. Crossland *The Future of Socialism* (1956).

In the first place the conventional analysis ignores the external costs associated with economic growth. Costs which are not internally met by the firm or the individual will not be taken into account in assessing the ratio of benefits to costs from any particular line of action. Such costs are, for instance, the pollution effects of manufacturing processes which make life unpleasant and sometimes hazardous for people. The argument is that if these unpleasant side-effects had to be offset by the firm then the ratio of benefits to costs would be considerably altered, and the distribution of economic resources correspondingly changed.[25]

It has been suggested that our measurement of economic growth, normally Gross or Net National Product, is inadequate. The statistics themselves may be lacking, but more important is that our definition of economic wealth is crude in the extreme. Any activity which gives rise to monetary transaction is said to increase N.N.P., while anything which does not have a monetary value does not enter into this calculation. For example a factory which is forced to instal machinery and employ personnel to reduce pollution is adding to the N.N.P., which is clearly something of a paradox. On the other hand, depreciation of the stock of natural amenities a country possesses, unlike the depreciation of man-made capital, is not included in the calculation, e.g. cutting down forests, eroding pasture land, etc.

The final argument is that the exponential increase in population and economic growth may well exhaust the world stock of raw materials in the not-too-distant future. Various investigations have been made to this effect, possibly the most controversial being the Club of Rome Report.[26] It is not our place to comment on these investigations at this time. What is certain, however, is that the growth debate continues unabated and will obviously intensify in the last quarter of the twentieth century.

ADDITIONAL READING

D. H. ALDCROFT AND P. FEARON *Economic Growth in Twentieth Century Britain* (1969)

D. H. ALDCROFT AND H. RICHARDSON *The British Economy, 1870–1939* (1969)

P. W. BARLEY AND D. W. SECKLER *Economic Growth and Environmental Decay* (New York 1972)

[25] Actions would normally have external benefits as well. In any case the market system fails to take account of these externalities, and to that extent resources are being less than optimally allocated.

[26] D. Meadowes (*et al.*) *The Limits to Growth* (1972).

W. BECKERMAN 'Why We Need Economic Growth' (*Lloyds Bank Review*, October 1971)

M. BLAUG *Economic Theory in Retrospect* (1964)

P. DEANE AND W. A. COLE *British Economic Growth, 1688–1959* (Cambridge 1962)

A. MADDISON 'How Fast Can Britain Grow?' (*Lloyds Bank Review*, January 1966); *Economic Growth in the West* (1964)

E. J. MISHAN *The Costs of Economic Growth* (1967)

I. SVENNILSON *Growth and Stagnation in the European Economy* (Geneva 1954)

CHAPTER 2

Population and Labour Supply

A constantly expanding labour supply was regarded during most of the nineteenth century as in the nature of things. The instinct of the population to reproduce was, according to Malthus, restrained only by the exercise of prudence or the necessity of subsistence; and in the majority of humans the former virtue was unhappily absent.[1] Thus the supply of food and the availability of employment were believed the principal determinants of demographic growth. By the 1870s, however, the first arrival in Britain of apparently inexhaustible supplies of imported American grain laid to rest, at least for a time, the fear that pressure on land would set in motion the law of diminishing returns; and the increase of international trade, the development of virgin agricultural land overseas, and the advance of industry at home, all proved conducive to high fertility. Contemporary economists did not doubt that production would continue to be boosted by the supply of labour; and later historians, whilst emphasizing that the impetus which population increase gave to economic growth was in some respects partial and inhibiting, have not questioned its importance.[2]

Since the First World War, however, economists have exhibited more disagreement on this issue. The size and composition of the British population has been suggested as one explanation of an allegedly unsatisfactory economic performance. Naturally enough, the details of the explanation have varied with the general assessment of current economic problems. And the hypothesis of demographic maladjustment has itself never been for long uncontested. Over the

[1] T. R. Malthus *Essay on Population* (1798). That the behaviour of the lower orders was never in reality so simple-minded is shown by E. A. Wrigley, 'Family Limitation in Pre-Industrial England' (*Econ. Hist. Rev.* 1966).

[2] Royal Commission on Population, Report of the Economics Committee (1946); S. G. Checkland, 'Growth and Progress: a nineteenth century view of Britain' (*Econ. Hist. Rev.* 1959–60); E. J. Hobsbawm, 'Custom, Wages and Workload in Nineteenth-Century Industry' (*Labouring Men* 1964); H. J. Habakkuk, *American and British Technology in the Nineteenth Century* (Cambridge 1962).

last fifty years, indeed, there have been regular fluctuations of opinion amongst economists as to whether the expansion of the labour force could advantageously be faster or slower than it has been in fact.

The argument was begun by Keynes in *The Economic Consequences of the Peace* (1920), published in the confused economic situation following the First World War, which revived, almost casually, the Malthusian spectre of overpopulation. In an increasingly industrialized world, Keynes suggested, the ability of the industrial nations to afford more and more imported foodstuffs might in the future diminish. He held out the prospect of too many manufactures competing for exchange with too few primary products – with the bleak consequences of declining export industries, a falling standard of living and a smaller national income. Keynes's pessimism was challenged at the time by W. H. Beveridge.[3] But the persistence of unemployment in the 1920s lent plausibility to his fears that the balance of the international market had shifted since the previous century. By 1930 Beveridge himself was writing, 'From the failure of real income per head to rise in the last twenty, perhaps the last thirty years, it looks as if a term was being set to the material progress of Britain and to her capacity for population, as if the economic balance of the world was changing against her.'[4] On rather different grounds, of the possibility of affording higher living standards and diminishing reliance on exports, Professor Reddaway also gave a cautious welcome to the prospect of a gradual population decline on the eve of the Second World War.[5]

Similar apprehensions were expressed after the war was over. In 1945 the Economics Committee of the Royal Commission on Population, confronted by the threat of an imbalance of payments of apparently irremediable proportions, wondered whether a static population might not be found economically desirable. 'If the balance of payments problem should prove to be one of long duration', it suggested, '. . . we may have cause not only to be glad that our numbers will soon cease to grow, but to welcome a considerable reduction.'[6] In the early 1950s, too, Professor Brinley Thomas noted that the worsening of British terms of trade since the

[3] *Economic Journal*, vol. 13, 1923.

[4] *Unemployment: A Problem of Industry* (1930 edn), p. 394.

[5] W. B. Reddaway *The Economics of a Declining Population* (1939).

[6] Report (1946), p. 15. Professor Reddaway was a member of the Committee: see the preface to the second (1945) edition of *Economics of a Declining Population* in this connection.

end of the previous decade made the outlook discouraging: the country could neither afford to lose labour by emigration nor to increase demand by immigration.[7] Since then, the continued growth of world population has posed wider social and political problems which have not allowed Malthus to be forgotten, even in times of national well-being.

Whilst arguments could always be found, throughout the years since 1918, for welcoming a decline in population growth, they rarely went uncontradicted for long. Keynes himself, having voiced fears of overpopulation in 1920, had so far changed his viewpoint by 1936 as to see the low rate of demographic expansion as a possible cause of the inadequate level of capital investment, and thereby of mass unemployment.[8] Falling population growth was also one of the key elements in the theory of secular stagnation which enjoyed a certain vogue in America as well as Britain in the inter-war years.[9] Later, one of the first economists to attempt to devise a general theory of economic growth, Professor Harrod, accepted that the rise of population in a developed economy would probably be slow, but argued that this was a long-term constraint on the expansion of its productive capacity.[10] And from less abstract and more political considerations the Royal Commission on Population, despite the previous findings of its Economics Committee, came down in 1949 in favour of encouraging higher fertility.[11] The introduction of family allowances, maternity benefits and the like showed that, for whatever reasons, the advocates of faster population growth had the upper hand in official circles.

Since the early 1950s, the prosperity of world trade and the continued international surplus of most primary products has enabled economists to ignore the effect of population size on terms of trade, and to treat the correction of the balance of payments simply as an aspect of the problem of improving British industrial productivity. Population, in other words, has once again been viewed, as in the nineteenth century, merely as a determinant of the labour supply. Yet the question of how far an increase in the labour factor of

[7] B. Thomas *Migration and Economic Growth* (Cambridge N.I.E.S.R. 1954), pp. 219, 222, 228–9.

[8] J. M. Keynes *General Theory of Employment, Interest and Money* (1936), pp. 307–9; see also p. 318.

[9] A. H. Hansen, 'Economic Progress and Declining Population Growth' (*American Economic Review*, March 1939).

[10] R. Harrod, 'An Essay in Dynamic Theory' (*Economic Journal*, vol. 49, 1939), and *Towards a Dynamic Economics* (1948).

[11] Report (Cmnd. 7695, 1949) p. 106.

production is a *sine qua non* of economic growth still provokes disagreement. On the one hand, Professors Lewis and Kindleberger (further developing Harrod's thesis) have given pride of place to the role of labour supply in accounting for economic growth. Kindleberger has argued at length that the different rates of expansion of West European economies since 1945 can be largely accounted for by the relative availability of labour, or by its rate of transfer from less to more productive uses.[12] On the other hand Professor Habakkuk, though admittedly talking about the nineteenth century, has suggested that the relative efficiency of American investment and technology in comparison with British was attributable to a *shortage* of appropriate labour reserves across the Atlantic and a state of surplus here.[13] And it is at least possible to argue that in the present century, too, a more gradual rise of population is more conducive to improvements in *per capita* productivity than a rapid increase. In any event, very few empirical studies in this field regard crude labour inputs (or capital inputs) as the major cause of growth in developed economies, in comparison with such secondary factors as technology, scale of production and allocation of resources.[14]

The importance given to the 'residual' in its various aspects has not diverted attention from the subject of the supply of labour, however, but rather shifted emphasis from the question of quantity to that of quality. The intrinsic efficiency of the workforce may be improved in a variety of ways so that, by virtue of greater skill, intelligence and physical fitness it becomes more productive. The currency of terms like 'human resources', 'human capital' and 'the productive function of labour' mark the emergence of a new interpretation of the significance of the labour factor in the economic system, which seeks to measure the historical effects of the development of education and other welfare services by their economic returns. Although the relationship of high welfare expenditure and faster economic growth is far from clear or consistent, there seems little doubt that some part in the progress of the economy during the twentieth century can be traced to this source – to the higher 'psychomotor and intellectual' qualities, to quote the terminology of the American Labour Department, which have been developed by 'investment in human beings'.[15]

[12] C. Kindleberger *Europe's Post-War Growth: The Role of Labour Supply* (Harvard 1967); W. A. Lewis *A Theory of Economic Growth* (1955).

[13] Habakkuk, op. cit.

[14] S. Kuznets *Modern Economic Growth* (1966), pp. 59, 82–3; Denison, 'Economic Growth' in Caves (ed.) *Britain's Economic Prospects* (1968).

[15] H. Correa *The Economics of Human Resources* (Amsterdam 1963); G. V.

To attempt to estimate the role of labour in promoting (or limiting) economic growth since 1918 is thus necessarily to tread upon ground mined by opposing theorists. Yet the incompatibility of previous accounts, especially in the British context, is perhaps explained in part by their differing historical terms of reference. It has been seen how economic opinion on the subject of population growth vacillated in sympathy with the character of immediate economic problems. On the other hand no empirical work and no theoretical model has yet given a convincing interpretation of the changing contribution of the labour force to the national economic performance throughout the whole period since 1918. The difficulties of such a task are considerable, for the period falls into two very dissimilar phases. The inter-war years were characterized by a falling birth-rate and at the same time by continuously high but sharply fluctuating unemployment levels. Since the last war the demand for labour has recovered, as for much of the period has the birth-rate too, so that a somewhat inelastic active population has been associated with a growing proportion of the economically inactive, and generally very full employment. Yet despite the sharp contrast between these two generations of the labour market, it has been shown that both periods saw economic growth of at any rate moderate proportions. Was there, then, an underlying similarity in the nature of the labour inputs in these two periods, which was concealed by the more striking but superficial transformation of the market situation? Or did the roughly comparable growth rate before and after the Second World War spring from altogether different sources in each case and labour make an uneven or transitory contribution? It will perhaps allow us to clarify these issues if we examine the labour market first in its unemployment and then in its full employment guise.

1918–1940

The inter-war years, as has been seen, were a time of abnormally low fertility, even of demographic crisis. In the early 1930s the birth-rate temporarily fell below 'replacement level', so that the generation which reached adulthood in the early 1950s was smaller than that which came of age in 1929–33. The birth-rate tended to recover slightly in the next few years, but not until the war was there a substantial increase in the fertility rate (coupled with some reduction

Rimlinger, 'Welfare Policy and Economic Development' *Journal of Economic History*, 26, 1966); *Journ. Pol. Econ.*, 'Investment in Human Beings' (Supplement, October 1962); O.E.C.D. *The Residual Factor and Economic Growth* (Paris 1964).

in the marriage rate). Patriotic despondency at the failure of the nation to show any strong desire to perpetuate itself was to help secure the introduction of family allowances in 1944, regarded by Beveridge as 'a signal of the national interest in children'. But the fall in the mean family size which had already occurred made a change in the age structure of the population and in the proportion of its retired relative to its employed members inevitable. Between 1891 and 1947 the average age of the British population rose by seven years; and between 1871 and 1947 the percentage of those over sixty-four years old increased from 4·8 to 10·4 of the total.

It is tempting to try and show a collinearity between these demographic trends and economic changes – and Professor Kindleberger is one economic historian to have noted the correspondence, at least up to the First World War, between the slackening of population growth and of economic growth. But it is less easy to make much of this point as regards the inter-war period. The continued downward movement of the birth-rate was then associated with a somewhat higher rate of economic growth than that of 1870–1914. Neither in the so-called 'Great Depression' of 1873–96, besides, nor in the 1920s and 1930s, were smaller families connected with a fall in national income per head. For most of these years, the majority of the population was enjoying rising real income and larger consumption.[16] And at least a part of the 'flight from maternity' can be explained by the upward social mobility of sections of the working class: the contraction of groups of traditionally very fertile workers like coal miners and agricultural labourers, and the proliferation of the 'unproductive clerk'. Thus it is equally hard to see economic growth between the wars as a consequence of past population change; or even to see unemployment and depression (the absence of faster growth) as the primary cause of current change.[17]

The population problem between the wars, in so far as it had economic consequences, existed in a European rather than an exclusively British context. The slackening birth-rates of the industrial nations of Western Europe, it could be argued, exacerbated the crisis of overproduction of primary products (especially food) which in turn disrupted the flow of goods between industrial and non-industrial nations in these years. Even in this wider perspective, however, it would be wrong to attribute the major responsibility for

[16] See Chapter 5.

[17] C. Kindleberger *Economic Growth in France and Britain* (1964). For a discussion of some aspects of the late-nineteenth century population trend, see J. A. Banks *Prosperity and Parenthood* (1954).

the decline of world trade after 1914 to the population factor. The increased output of agricultural produce and raw materials was initially the effect of wartime circumstances, later reinforced by technological advances. It is difficult to conceive that a problem of world surplus in these commodities could have been avoided even given the continuance of high birth-rates. And the failure to contain or correct this problem was, of course, the result of national commercial and monetary policies which had little or nothing to do with population movements.

As far as Britain was concerned, the falling birth-rate did threaten, in the long run, to constrict the growth of the labour force. And other social changes, too, moved in the same direction. The migration of labour from agriculture into industry, which had considerably raised the *per capita* productivity of the employed population throughout the nineteenth century, was tailing off after 1914. The minimum school-leaving age was advanced to fourteen and part-time employment of school-children abolished by the Education Act of 1918, prompting loud complaints from Lancashire textile manufacturers in particular at their deprivation of boy labour. And the employment of women, which had increased dramatically during the First World War, fell off almost as much immediately afterwards.[18] The continued rise in the marriage rate between the wars probably exercised a mildly adverse influence on the further recruitment of women in peacetime.

TABLE 11

Population and the Labour Force, 1911–68

Great Britain	Pop.	Labour force: Male	Female	Total
		Thousands		
1911	40,831	12,927	5,424	18,351
1921	42,769	13,656	5,701	19,357
1931	44,795	14,790	6,265	21,055
1951	48,918	16,007	7,419	23,426
1968	53,781	16,322	8,936	25,258

SOURCES *Abstract of Labour Statistics, 1919–33*; *Registrar-General's Statistical Review for England and Wales, 1968*; *Employment and Productivity Gazette*, January 1970.

Despite these trends, however, the expansion of the *employed* population after the first war was not significantly checked. The fall

[18] 1,200,000 women were added to the labour force in 1914–18, but the net increase of the years 1913–20 was only a little over 200,000 (Report of the Committee on the Employment of Women, Cmd. 9164, 1918).

in the fertility rate was beginning to act as a brake on the absolute growth of the labour force only towards the end of this period; and at no time between 1919 and 1940 did the number of occupied males (a statistical series more sensitive to changes in the crude birth-rate than that of the whole occupied population) cease to grow. Chiefly because of the increase in the number of retired people, the adult participation rate – the ratio of economically active members to the total population aged over fourteen – declined slightly in these years. The decline was only slight, however, since the age groups forming the active population probably benefited as much from improvements in health and advances in medical knowledge as those over sixty-five: between 1901 and 1911, and 1930 and 1935, the life expectancy of newly-born children rose from forty-eight and a half to fifty-nine years. Moreover the participation rate of the population as a whole rose, thanks to the diminishing proportion formed by those under fifteen. Finally, from being a country of emigration in the 1920s, Britain began in the 1930s to attract more people from abroad than it exported. A combination of restrictive immigration policies in Commonwealth countries, political tyranny in Europe, and a shortage of native domestic servants produced a positive migration balance between 1931 and 1939.[19]

That there was no problem of simple labour shortage in the inter-war years is of course decisively demonstrated by the endurance of heavy unemployment. At its peak, in 1921 and 1931, unemployment affected almost a fifth of the insured population. At its nadir, in 1924, 1928–9, and 1936, it still kept 9 to 10 per cent of eligible workers on benefit or assistance. The problem was most serious, as is well known, in the regions of 'outer Britain' – South Wales, central Scotland, northern and north-western England. It was here that the most depressed industries were concentrated: coal mining from about 1925, cotton textiles from about 1929, steel and shipbuilding throughout the whole period.[20] It was here, in consequence, that the so-called

[19] Census of England and Wales, 1961, Preliminary Report. Three out of five labour permits granted to foreign immigrants in the 1930s were for domestic servants. It is worth considering whether the decline in this occupation after the First World War did not to some extent offset the reduction in the transfers from agriculture to industry. The number of men engaged in 'domestic offices and personal services' fell by 83,000 between 1911 and 1921, the number of women by 282,000 (B. R. Mitchell and P. Deane *Abstract of British Historical Statistics*, p. 60). For the distress aroused among middle-class employers of servants by this defection, see Women's Advisory Committee on Domestic Servants, *Report* (Cmd. 67, 1919), and *Report of Inquiry into the Effect of the Unemployment Insurance Act on the Supply of Domestics* (1923).

[20] Immediately after the collapse of the post-war boom the heavy engineering

'long unemployed' were congregated: men who had been idle for years rather than weeks or months. 63 per cent of those unemployed in the Rhondda fell into this category by 1936, 56 per cent at Crook – compared with 11 per cent in Leicester, 7 per cent in Deptford. In north Britain and Wales as a whole, long unemployment among the insured population was six times heavier than in the south and Midlands.

TABLE 12

National and Regional Unemployment

	Percentage of insured population, U.K.			
	1913–14	1937	1950	1968
U.K.	3·8	10·4	1·6	2·5
London	7·3	8·2	1·1	1·6
S.E.	4·0	6·1		
S.W.	5·1	7·1	1·5	2·7
W. Midlands	3·3	6·0	0·4	1·9
E. Midlands	2·7		0·8	2·3
N.W.	3·3	12·9	1·4	2·3
N.E.	2·7	9·2	2·7	4·9
Northern	2·4	19·1		
Scotland	2·1	15·2	3·0	3·7
Wales	2·3	24·3	3·4	4·0
N. Ireland	7·0	26·2	6·3	7·5

SOURCES Beveridge *Unemployment in a Free Society*; *British Labour Statistics, 1886–1968.*

The prolongation of unemployment provides incontrovertible evidence of the adequacy of the labour force to achieve a higher economic growth rate than was in fact obtained in the inter-war period. The argument was stated in simple fashion by, for instance, the famous Liberal election programme of 1929:[21]

> Side by side, we have a great army of workers longing for employment and a multitude of tasks waiting to be done. . . . Cannot we use this great labour force to improve our roads, house or re-house our workers, develop our power resources, drain our lands? . . . Nothing, we think, will strike the future historian more than the *waste* of our present unemployment policy.

industry was also abnormally depressed, as the result of the contraction of war-time demand; but it had reduced its surplus labour pool to 'normal' proportions by the end of the decade.

[21] *We can Conquer Unemployment* (1929), pp. 7–8.

And the preceding economic inquiry on which this programme was based pointed out the additional indirect economic penalties inflicted by unemployment:[22]

> Its effects include the handicap which the necessity of providing for the unemployed imposes upon industry; the slackening of effort on the part of wage-earners due to the belief that – whatever economists may say – there is only a limited amount of work, and to go workless is to go hungry; and the contraction of the demand for goods in the home industry which inevitably follows a shrinkage of wage-earners' incomes.

This view, it should be noticed, emphasized total economic output rather than output *per capita*, as the main index of growth. And it is now conventional wisdom that a large proportion of the unemployed could have been absorbed and aggregate economic production by the application of Keynesian policies. But whether the elimination of the jobless would have raised the productivity of British industry is a more difficult question. There is little point in asking how fuller employment would have affected the marginal productivity of labour, for too many imponderables are involved in such a calculation. It can only be assumed that some gains would have been registered in some industries by working at fuller capacity. On the other hand it is naïve to suppose, in the conditions existing in the 1920s and 1930s, that a large reserve of labour was synonymous with inefficiency. The industries yielding the most impressive series of input–output ratios in this period, showing the greatest advances in the economical use of labour, include some which had suffered and continued to suffer from the heaviest unemployment. Coal mining provides a striking example; the output of coal fell by 12·9 per cent between 1923 and 1937, whilst the occupied labour force fell by 34·2 per cent. The improvement of productivity was here more important than any other single cause – falling exports, industrial warfare, competition from other forms of energy – in creating redundancies in the industry. The results of rationalization in shipbuilding and textiles were scarcely less impressive. These industries had, of course, most room for improvement; but this does not affect the point that in such cases the growth of output per head was associated with reduced employment. In relation to such structurally declining trades the Chairman of the T.U.C. General Council had good reason for saying, of rationalization, 'I do not see what we can

[22] Liberal Party *Britain's Industrial Future* (1928), p. 267.

get out of it except a lot of unemployment which we are not going to be able to absorb.'[23]

This is not by any means to suggest, however, that unemployment was in general connected with higher productivity; it was also indirectly the cause of at least a measure of industrial inefficiency. In the first place, high unemployment tended to foster higher underemployment: it encouraged labour to attach itself more inseparably to jobs that were casual, seasonal or part-time in character. Secondly, there may be some truth in the observation of contemporary public inquiries, that the fear of idleness encouraged workmen to enter jobs for which they were unsuited. The example of the public works projects of the inter-war years is perhaps extreme and atypical; but in a great many industries at this time, labour turnover was rapid and employment unstable, even against a background of relative growth and prosperity, for reasons which have never been clarified. Most important, however, heavy unemployment was one factor influencing the long-term changes in the occupational structure of the population – and influencing them in ways that were sometimes unhelpful to economic growth. For workers and the children of workers who sought after security during the depression looked less often to the growth points of manufacturing industry than to service and white-collar occupations, where they were protected from disturbance not just by the natural expansion of the tertiary sector, but sometimes by the defences of status and the operation of Parkinson's Law as well. The insured workpeople employed in 'consumer services' increased by 1,185,000 between 1924 and 1937, whilst the net expansion of the labour force in the whole of manufacturing industry was no more than 530,000. The period between the wars belonged, from this perspective, to the clerk, the typist and the shop assistant on the one hand, the bartender and the bookie's runner on the other. And it was their occupations, in general, which used labour most wastefully and least productively. Services as a whole actually had a negative residual factor in the years 1924 to 1937.[24] These indeed formed the real 'sheltered industries' of the time.

[23] Macmillan Committee on Finance and Industry, Mins. of Evid. Vol. i; Q. 4668.

[24] J. A. Dowie, 'Growth in the Inter-war Period: Some More Arithmetic' (*Econ. Hist. Rev.* 21, 1968); R. C. O. Matthews, 'Some Aspects of Post-war Growth in the British Economy in Relation to Historical Experience' (*Manchester Statistical Soc. Transacs.*, 1964–5). For evidence on the expansion of white-collar occupations, see D. Lockwood *The Blackcoated Worker* (2nd edn., 1966).

What has so far been studied is the effect of inadequate labour demand, both on aggregate industrial output and on productivity. But what of the effect of labour supply? Whilst there was certainly no absolute labour shortage in the inter-war period, there may have been other shortcomings in the quality of labour available, which hampered the performance of the economy. This aspect of the inter-war employment situation has been little considered since it became popular to attribute the economic difficulties of the period to deficiency of demand. But perhaps the other side of the question is worth some review.

The problem of labour supply was regarded in the 1930s, however, from the angle which now seems least promising and relevant: the angle of labour mobility. From the late 1920s successive governments were attracted by the view that the transference of labour from depressed areas to prosperous ones would boost the economy and alleviate unemployment. Unemployment had created stagnant pools of manpower – had, perhaps, discouraged the fluidity which had been a sign of economic health in the past.[25] To restore freedom of movement would ensure the competitiveness of the labour market, and thus prevent some of the misallocation of labour which has already been noticed.

The inertia of the labour force, however, was an insignificant handicap to economic recovery. Workers did not move in the 1920s and 1930s (least of all under official auspices) because it did not seem worthwhile to leave areas of heavy unemployment for areas of moderate unemployment. To urge them to do otherwise was 'like running excursion trains to a football match which is not being played'.[26] In addition, mobility on a large scale resembled regional bloodletting; in the case of the one area from which there was a major exodus of population, South Wales, it is arguable that the

[25] It is difficult to obtain evidence on migration trends in this period from the census, but it seems probable that both short- and long-distance movement did decline from about the time of the First World War (D. Friedlander, R. J. Roshier, 'Internal Migration in England and Wales, 1851–1951' (*Pop. Stud.* 19, 1965–66). The pattern varied from region to region, however, and this variation is even more obvious in regard to migration caused by unemployment, as distinct from other factors: see G. H. Daniel, 'Some factors Affecting the Movement of Labour' (*Oxf. Econ. Pap.* 3, 1940). For further discussion of this subject, see the series of articles entitled 'Studies in the Mobility of Labour' by H. Makower, J. Marschak and H. W. Robinson (*Oxf. Econ. Pap.* 1, 2 and 4, 1938–40). The data found here tend to support the view that industrial mobility was relatively low in the inter-war period, and especially at the height of the depression, in 1931–3.

[26] *We Can Conquer Unemployment*, p. 9.

outcome was economically as well as socially deleterious.[27] Finally, the case for transference assumed that the employers of Inner Britain would prefer migrant to native workers on the sole grounds of skill and quality. But the Industrial Transference Board itself noted a widespread apprehension among management that unemployed coal miners, for instance, would import into the districts receiving them 'contagious elements of unrest and disturbance'.[28] A few years later, Lord Nuffield did in fact tell his local employment exchange that his firm would accept no more Welsh coalworkers after experiencing the militancy of those they had already engaged. In any case, it seemed illogical to conclude that employers who recruited labour haphazardly under conditions of relatively low unemployment would recruit it systematically when the proportion of the jobless rose further.

In other respects, however, the supply of labour was more susceptible to measures of practical amelioration. To begin with, social reformers had long talked of the need for reorganizing the labour market, for eliminating the worst centres of casual employment like the docks, and for increasing the powers and effectiveness of the employment exchanges.[29] Although measures of this kind might have done little to reduce unemployment they would at least have tackled that problem of 'residual' labour, the existence of marginal elements in the working population only partially integrated into a developed economic system, which continued to be numbered among the out-of-work throughout the inter-war years. But little or nothing was done in this direction. The employment exchanges in particular were denied any compulsory authority, even to deal with notorious casual industries. In 1921 the Geddes Economy Committee actually proposed their abolition; and although they survived and even increased their activities in subsequent years, they never managed to fill more than about 20 per cent of job vacancies.

Linked with the lack of organization in the labour market was the lack of skill in the labour force. The relative predominance of unskilled workers among the unemployed was fully appreciated in the inter-war years. In 1930 almost one-quarter of the male unemployed fell into the category of general unskilled labourers (excluding build-

[27] South Wales was the only region in Britain to suffer a reduction not just in total population but in insured population, between 1923 and 1937.

[28] Industrial Transference Board, *Report*, p. 10.

[29] The first comprehensive proposals on these lines were put forward by the Majority and Minority Reports of the Royal Commission on the Poor Laws in 1909.

ing and dock labourers); and in 1937 almost two-thirds of the jobless in mining, engineering, shipbuilding and building were unskilled. 30·5 per cent of all unskilled workers were unemployed in June 1931 as compared with 14·4 per cent of the skilled and semi-skilled.[30] Yet clear though it was that unskilled labour was in relatively less demand than skilled, very little was done between the wars to promote industrial training. In 1920 the Ministry of Labour found that in a sample of 907 firms, 671 made no provision at all for the instruction of the labour they recruited. A year later it reported that only 20 per cent of boys under twenty-one were getting any form of training in industry; and in the mid-1920s, even in the apprenticed trades no more than one-fifth of employers provided this mode of instruction.[31] The government, for its part, set up twenty adult training centres of different sorts by 1930–1, whilst Junior Instruction Centres under the auspices of Local Education Authorities catered for some 74,000 teenagers in 1930. But many of the courses offered at these institutions were of dubious value, and certainly neither unemployed workers nor trade unions were inclined to welcome them. Probably the most useful facilities available in these years were the day-release classes provided by local technical colleges, where attendance figures rose from 26,000 to 42,000 between 1932 and 1938.[32] The opportunity to guarantee some vocational education to the whole of the working population had been lost right at the beginning of this period, however, with the abandonment of the 'continuation' classes envisaged in the Fisher Education Act of 1918.

Even this brief consideration of the character of the labour supply is enough to demonstrate the point that the problem of labour efficiency between the wars was not simply an aspect of the problem of unemployment. Although the inadequacy of labour demand was a grave economic handicap, a brake on the growth of output and sometimes on the improvement of productivity, its correction would not in itself have sufficed to realize anything like the full potential of the country's labour resources. Other factors adversely and unduly affecting the participation rate of the occupied population would still have had to be tackled: underemployment in some casual trades and services; continued structural unemployment in some industries;

[30] G. Routh *Occupation and Pay in Great Britain, 1906–60* (1965), pp. 126–7; S. Pollard *Development of the British Economy 1914–67* (1969).

[31] E. M. Burns *British Unemployment Programmes, 1920–38* (Washington 1941).

[32] O. M. V. Argles *South Kensington to Robbins* (1964), p. 69.

and the burdens, not hitherto mentioned, of ill-health and industrial stoppages.[33] The quality and productivity of the labour force could likewise have been substantially improved, even within the limits of the accepted welfare principles of the time.[34] One incidental consequence of the affliction of unemployment was to distract attention from other social ailments, less urgent but in the long run equally significant, which in the inter-war years suffered unfortunate neglect.

1940–1968

The Second World War was a watershed, dividing a period of unemployment from a period of labour shortage and, less sharply, a period of rapid growth in the active population from a period marked by the relatively faster growth of the inactive population. This combination of circumstances has naturally suggested the possibility that economic expansion has been hampered by a scarcity of manpower.[35] But how great was this scarcity, and how irremediable?

The population trends of this period changed significantly from those of the previous generation. Because of the low birth-rates of the 1920s and 1930s, the adult population after the Second World War grew fairly slowly until the mid-1960s. The number of births began markedly to increase again during the war, however, and the increase revived during the 1950s, lasting until 1965. Together with the growing numbers in retirement and the extension of full-time education among adolescents, this had the effect of weighting the proportion of dependants relative to the proportion of those occupied. From 1958, the annual rate of increase of the total population exceeded the rate of increase in the labour force. And for a brief period between 1965 and mid-1968 the size of the working population declined absolutely.

These changes in the labour supply might have been still more pronounced, but the contraction in the number of adult males entering the labour market was offset by the expansion in the number

[33] For industrial stoppages, see Chapter 4; for ill-health, see P.E.P. *Report on the British Health Services* (1937). The number of reported cases of industrial diseases reached a peak around 1930 – *Annual Report of H.M. Inspector of Factories on Industrial Health, 1966* (Cmnd. 3359, 1967), pp. 30–1.

[34] The contribution of education to industrial performance had been a commonplace since the 1860s; and the broader principles of the 'human capital' school were present in an earlier and cruder form in the thinking of 'social imperialists' from before the First World War (see B. Semmel *Imperialism and Social Reform*).

[35] Kindleberger *Europe's Post-War Growth*; N. Kaldor *Causes of the Slow Rate of Economic Growth of the U.K.* (Cambridge 1966).

of married women in employment, and the arrival of immigrants from overseas. The proportion of women in the occupied population, having remained more or less unchanged during the inter-war period, rose substantially during and after the Second World War. Between 1951 and 1966 the female labour force in Britain increased by 20·9 per cent where the male labour force grew by only 5·4 per cent.

It was married women who were chiefly responsible for the disparity, for they formed 42·3 per cent of the total female workforce in 1951 and 54·6 per cent in 1965. Numerically, immigrants made a much less important contribution to the labour force, but their relative concentration in high employment areas made them a strategic group (discounting their social and political impact). The level of immigration between 1951 and 1961 stood slightly higher than the decennial level in 1931–51, and was especially high in the three years or so prior to the Commonwealth Immigration Act of 1962. Since then, Britain has again become a net exporter of population.

These infiltrators of the male and Anglo-Saxon working population, however, have not fully compensated for the unborn Englishmen that they replaced. Married women workers are somewhat less mobile, industrially and geographically, than their husbands; certainly, for a variety of social and personal reasons, they are less skilled and versatile. As a result the occupational structure of the female labour force has changed relatively little despite its growth in size. Between 1951 and 1961 women sought jobs chiefly in those fields where they were already strongly entrenched: commerce and finance, clerical work, personal and professional services. Thus in this decade the proportion of women to men increased from 55·7 per cent to 60·1 per cent in the clerical occupations, but declined in every other non-manual occupation as well as in skilled manufacturing trades. Immigrant workers have also, for a variety of obvious reasons, been channelled largely into unskilled and service work.

There are other reasons, besides the misuse of female and coloured workers, for arguing that labour has been employed less effectively than it might have been since the Second World War. Despite the persistence of labour shortage in the country as a whole, a certain amount of regional unemployment has continued. National unemployment rates have been kept down, partly by the effect of government policy but largely by the volume of private investment. Furthermore, the most flagrant forms of casual and irregular hiring have disappeared before the same combination of official pressure and entrepreneurial prudence.[36] But that problem of 'depressed

[36] R. C. O. Matthews, 'Why has Britain had Full Employment since the War?'

areas' which was so familiar in the 1930s has, in a modified form, survived. Regional unemployment statistics between 1961 and 1968 point the accusing finger in the same direction as before, at Wales, Scotland, Northern Ireland and north-east England. Whether the general level of unemployment were high or low during this period, the development areas continued to record rates 60 to 100 per cent above the national average. And although the burden is manifestly much more tolerable than it was before the war, the disparity between areas of high and low unemployment has been frequently of a higher order than it was during the depression. The structural problems of old industries, the concentration of industries sensitive to cyclical fluctuations, and the relative lack of secure service occupations, all contribute to this situation. And what is equally noticeable is the unchanged aspect of the unemployed themselves, whose physiognomy has altered little since the 1930s. Joblessness and redundancy still affect the unskilled and old disproportionately. Approximately half of those out of work in 1958–61, and the large majority of those suffering from more than temporary idleness, were unskilled labourers. But in the case of workers made redundant in the early 1960s, both in the Midlands car industry and in the railway workshops of Manchester and Darlington, it was age rather than skill which proved the main barrier to finding new work.

Redundancy, unemployment, and the uneven regional pattern of industrial decline and development have prompted continued discussion of the question of labour mobility. Although transference has ceased to be regarded as a solution to such problems, the Ministry of Labour retained the power under the Employment and Training Act of 1948 and the Local Employment Act of 1960 to give financial assistance to the movement of labour where it seemed economically desirable – mainly for training purposes. The power was not much used, but the government has at the very least remained interested in discovering the extent to which labour was prepared to change occupation and residence. The evidence is not very encouraging to those who believe in the value of geographical mobility as a stimulus to economic progress. Sample inquiries suggest that, in the fifteen years 1945–59, 36 per cent of the population moved far enough to change their local authority, but only 11 per cent moved between regions. Both the frequency and distance of mobility varied directly with social status. There is little evidence that long-distance mobility

(*Economic Journal*, vol. 78, 1968); Alan Bullock *Ernest Bevin*, vol. ii (1967), pp. 58–9. Employment exchanges have not improved their pre-war record, however: see A. F. Young *Social Services in British Industry* (1968), p. 18.

among the workforce was any longer influenced, as before the war, by differential unemployment rates between Inner and Outer Britain. A later official survey presented a similar picture, though indicating a higher than average exchange of population within the constituent areas of the south and east of England. But only 16 to 18 per cent of all such changes of address were prompted by considerations of employment.

The extent of industrial mobility (not necessarily involving a change of address) was probably somewhat higher. The same official inquiry found that 44 per cent of their male respondents had taken new jobs between 1953 and 1963, although probably fewer than half had changed their industrial affiliation. Movement between jobs and industries had been significantly higher in the immediate post-war period, however, at least in the London area. The specific case-studies of redundancy in Birmingham and elsewhere also tend to show that the termination of contracts can have fairly considerable effects in directing the labour concerned into new forms of employment.

In general, however, redeploying the labour force for the purpose of encouraging greater productivity has proved no less difficult since 1945 than before 1939. Certainly it can have done little to solve the acute shortage of skilled workers, among whom mobility was less high than among other grades. What is more, between 1951 and 1961 the total number of skilled workers in the labour force fell by half a million, while the number of unskilled rose by 400,000. Changes of job could do little or nothing to affect this trend. If anything redundancies enforced by deflationary government policies probably had adverse effects in this respect, at least in the short term, frequently leading unemployed workers to take jobs of inferior skill to those they previously held. The misuse of immigrant and women's labour has already been noticed. The hoarding of skilled labour by manufacturing industries and the underemployment of unskilled and service workers were still held to be prevalent in the early 1960s – and the effect of the Selective Employment Tax, the introduction of computers, and the conduct of productivity bargaining with trade unions on these practices has still not been measured.[37]

[37] Productivity in retailing did increase faster in 1965–8 than it has done in the period 1957–66, though this could be credited to the repeal of Resale Price Maintenance as well as to the S.E.T. (W. B. Reddaway *Effects of the Selective Employment Tax* (1970), pp. 66–8. For productivity bargaining, see below. pp. 88–90.

In the absence of convenient short cuts, the simple but expensive solution of increasing labour productivity by producing more intelligent and better trained labour has still much to commend it. Recent economic research, both theoretical and empirical, has tended to lay increased stress on the importance of education to the process of growth.[38] One estimate attributed about 12 per cent of the total increase in national income in Britain between 1950 and 1962 to this factor. Elsewhere, it has been suggested that the rate of return on recent expenditure on secondary education in Britain was roughly 13 per cent, that on higher education 14 per cent—calculated on the basis of the increased incomes which its beneficiaries enjoy as a result.[39]

The assumptions behind this arithmetic have been criticized;[40] but the advocates of education can point to general reasons for asserting its importance. Leaving aside the vexed question of how far higher incomes have resulted from increasing intelligence and skill in the labour force, it is obviously true that the technical and operational adaptability of the workforce is improved by education. The rate of industrial innovation and the supply of managerial talent may also plausibly be linked with its provision. Similarly, education has been shown to be connected with the degree of labour mobility. And what these observations seem to imply is that the *indirect* effects of education, in conjunction with other economic processes, may well be at least as important as its direct effects on personal remuneration.

In this field too, however, the achievements of the post-war period have been patchy. The 1944 Education Act was less radical in its execution than in its conception. And throughout the subsequent period, progress in the sphere of higher education—the training of scientists, technologists and technicians in particular—has tended to be more rapid than in other sectors. The number of university graduates in science and technology increased from about 5,000 in 1938/9 to about 17,000 in 1960 and 26,000 in 1968. On the other hand, between 1931 and 1961 the *average* length of full-time education amongst the male school population as a whole increased by

[38] E. Denison *Sources of Economic Growth* (Washington 1962), chap. 7; and *Why Growth Rates Differ?* (Washington 1967); T. Schultz, 'Investment in Human Capital' (*A.E.R.* 1961).

[39] Denison, 'Economic Growth', in Caves (ed.) *Britain's Economic Prospects*, p. 244; D. Henderson-Stewart, 'Estimate of the Rate of Return to Education in Great Britain' (*Manchester School* 1965).

[40] T. Balogh and P. Streeten, 'The Coefficient of Ignorance' (*Bull. Oxf. Univ. Instit. Stats.*, 25, 1963).

only just over a year, from 8·85 to 9·94 years, a rise almost wholly accounted for by the raising of the school leaving age in 1947. This is not to suggest that the expenditure on tertiary education was disproportionate to need or demand, for it came in response to an obvious shortage of qualified scientists (and graduates in general) and was intended to bring Britain into line with other countries in an area where she had fallen furthest behind. The increased expenditure at primary and secondary school level, however, did little but keep pace with the growth of population, although it was here, among the age group of eleven to sixteen, that the chief 'wastage' of talent was shown to occur.[41] But not until the past few years has the reform of secondary education quickened in pace.

Industrial training has advanced even more slowly and unsteadily. Despite the development of easier and more *ad hoc* methods of training in such expanding industries as vehicle manufacture, there was, as we have seen, a reduction in the number of skilled workers during the 1950s. The main reason for this would seem to be the traditionalist and inflexible character of much formal industrial instruction, especially by apprenticeship, and the relative indifference of many firms (especially large ones) to their responsibilities in this respect. Although in the past they engaged in perennial conflict over issues of apprenticeship ratios and the like, since World War II it appears that 'employers and trade unions have found a *modus vivendi* as regards apprenticeship which . . . reduces current productivity and trammels the flexibility of the economy'.[42] The first attempts of government to encourage training, through the Education and Training Act of 1948, were based on voluntaryist principles, and predictably had most impact on industries with a good established record. Not until March 1964 were more imperative measures adopted, in the Industrial Training Act, which compelled all firms either to make provision for training or to contribute to a levy for this purpose. The success of this legislation, however, depends on the activities of training boards which are still in their infancy. Their efforts are being supplemented by the widening operations of Government Training Centres, existing on a small scale since 1917

[41] E. Denison, 'Measuring the Contribution of Education to Economic Growth', in O.E.C.D. *The Residual Factor in Economic Growth*; S. Harris, 'Public Expenditure on Education', in L. Reifman (ed.) *Financing of Education for Economic Growth* (O.E.C.D. Paris 1964); *Fifteen to Eighteen*, Report of the Central Advisory Council for Education (1959); A. Little, J. Westergaard, 'The Trend of Class Differentials in Educational Opportunity in England and Wales' (*British Journal of Sociology* 1964).

[42] K. Liepmann *Apprenticeship* (1960), p. 196.

but expanded in 1958 and 1966. The refusal of some trade unions to accept their graduates as members no doubt indicates the kind of problems which official schemes of this kind face, and still must overcome.[43]

Conclusion

The perfect labour supply, like economic man, does not exist. The labour force in Britain, for part or all of the period since 1918, has revealed evident deficiencies, either of quality or of quantity. These were problems which caused little disquiet until the end of the nineteenth century, although the general economic *quality* of the labour force during the first industrial revolution was manifestly much lower than it had become by 1918. But unemployment between the wars, and more especially the stresses of full employment since 1945, have focused attention on this subject, albeit on different aspects of it. Restrictive labour practices, transference and redeployment, education and training, trade union reform, incomes policy, have all emerged as major concerns of economic and industrial policy.

Is this preoccupation justified, economically speaking? If we start from the premise that crude labour inputs are the most important aspect of labour's contribution to the productive process, then there is little that *policy* can achieve. But this assumption has been attacked, both on theoretical and empirical grounds. There is no necessary antithesis between a limited supply of labour and a rapid rate of economic growth. The application of labour has certainly been statistically less significant than capital investment or (in some sectors) the residual as an explanation of growth in mature economies. And this factor does not appear to have been the most important point of difference between Britain and other countries (whether faster- or slower-growing) since 1918. Moreover, in Britain itself, considering the whole period from 1873 to 1968, changes in the size of the active population and of the gross national product have been obviously discrepant. If there is a connection between labour and growth, it is not a simple one to establish.

The starting point of almost any labour policy must therefore be the assumption that the quality of the labour supply and the efficiency with which it is employed are potentially more important than the simple factor of size. Productivity is not a function of inputs of

[43] G. Williams *Recruitment of Skilled Trades* (1957); Royal Comm. on Trade Unions and Employers Associations *Report;* G. Terry Page *The Industrial Training Act and After* (1967).

labour and capital, and the 'residual' consists of more than 'technical change'.[44] The capacities of the labour force are embodied in the residual too, as the outcome of its conjunction with many other factors in the economic process.

We are still at the early stages of validating and applying such principles, and analysing their operation. But if these qualitative factors have any significance, then the deficiencies in the labour force which have been noticed in this chapter must have acted as a brake on the expansion of the economy. For although in Britain the labour market situation altered so drastically during the Second World War, the skills and adaptability of the labour force changed much less markedly. Thus even during the later 1930s, when national unemployment remained abnormally high, certain shortages of *skilled* labour could occur in particular industrial bottlenecks. More generally, it is evident that both before and after the war the available labour supply was often deployed inefficiently. Although the scarcity of manpower since 1945 has helped bring about the elimination of some aspects of this inefficiency (casual employment), it has had less influence on others (systematic overtime), and has itself given rise to new abuses (hoarding of skilled workers). The remedying of unemployment between the wars might not in itself have led to any marked improvement in labour utilization; a larger influx of labour into the post-war market would similarly have left many of this species of problem unsolved.

ADDITIONAL READING

W. H. BEVERIDGE *Unemployment: A Problem of Industry* (1930); *Full Employment in A Free Society* (new edn, 1960)

D. V. GLASS, *Population Policies and Movements* (1967 reprint)

A. HARRIS AND R. CLAUSEN *Labour Mobility in Great Britain, 1953–63* (1966)

H. R. KAHN *Repercussions of Redundancy* (1964)

R. C. O. MATTHEWS 'Some Aspects of Post-War Unemployment in the Light of Historical Experience' (*Manchester Statistical Society Transacs.* 1964–5)

MINISTRY OF LABOUR, Manpower Reports: I *Patterns of the Future* (1964); II *Occupational Changes 1951–61* (1967)

F. R. OLIVER 'Inter-Regional Migration, 1951–61' (*Journ. of Roy. Stat. Society*, Ser. A 127, 1964)

P.E.P. *Population Policy in Great Britain* (1948)

PILGRIM TRUST *Men Without Work* (1937)

ROYAL COMMISSION ON THE DISTRIBUTION OF THE INDUSTRIAL POPULATION *Report* (1939)

J. SAVILLE *Rural Depopulation in England and Wales, 1851–1951* (1957)

D. WEDDERBURN *Redundancy and the Railwaymen* (1965)

[44] Chapter 3.

CHAPTER 3

Capital, Technology and Growth

Economic theorists from Adam Smith to the present day have emphasized the importance of capital accumulation in the process of economic growth. It is ostensibly easy to see why capital should be given this primary place. The other factors of production, land and labour, are determined by 'natural' forces and in any one period are likely to be in inelastic supply. Thus economic expansion would inevitably lead to diminishing returns. The onset of diminishing returns could, however, be postponed through the application of more and more units of capital. But the simple addition of more units of capital by itself would only postpone the onset of the Stationary State. For the importance of capital investment as a permanent influence on growth we must also consider its indirect or secondary effect, on what, in the nineteenth century, was called the 'State of the Arts', or in modern terms of education and technological change. Even though nineteenth-century economists tended to underestimate the sheer scope of technical change, they were nevertheless aware of its place in the scheme of economic development.

As countries become industrialized, and presumably more capital intensive, the relative importance of investment will increase. Though the marginalist school of economists which emerged in the last quarter of the nineteenth century tended to emphasize the comparatively static aspect of the economic system, capital accumulation still retained its primary place. However, the precise nature of the relationship between investment and growth remained vague, and not until the 1930s and 1940s was there any systematic attempt to discover what was the relationship. This attempt is associated with the names of R. Harrod and E. Domar, and though their work has been superseded by more sophisticated theories, it is still worth our while to look briefly at this earlier seminal work.

In the Harrod/Domar model, investment plays a key role in the growth process. The sheer fact of investment has a two-fold effect. On the supply side it adds to the productive potential of the economy, and on the demand side it increases effective aggregate demand via the Keynesian multiplier process. In equilibrium planned saving must equal planned investment, but the net investment of one period adds to the capacity of the following period. Thus to maintain the full utilization of economic resources, aggregate demand of the next period will also have to exceed that of the current period.

Under the assumptions of the model, of a fixed capital coefficient and no technical change, capacity is some fixed function of investment. Thus if the capital coefficient $= \sigma$

$$\Delta Y = \sigma I$$

where ΔY is the potential increase in real income. Thus potential real income will increase at the same rate as investment.

From Keynesian analysis it can be shown that

$$\Delta Y = \frac{1}{\alpha} \Delta I$$

where α is the marginal propensity to save. Thus for equilibrium growth

$$\sigma I = \frac{\Delta I}{\alpha}$$

$$\frac{\Delta I}{I} = \theta\alpha$$

Capacity growth must equal the growth in aggregate demand, which is determined by the propensity to save and the productivity of capital. From this emerges the paradox of the model. If actual investment is lower than that warranted, aggregate income will increase less than capacity; resources will be made unemployed, the incentive for further investment reduced. If on the other hand actual investment is higher than warranted, aggregate income will increase faster than capacity and investment will be found to be inadequate. In either case the key to the growth process is the level of investment.[1]

Towards the middle of the nineteenth century Britain had clearly emerged as the leading industrial nation in the world, and with its policy of free trade was the fulcrum of the international trading system. To maintain the flow of commodities Britain had undertaken vast foreign lending programmes. The London capital market was

[1] All modern textbooks on macro-economics will have a section on the Harrod/Domar growth model, e.g. E. Shapiro *Macroeconomic Analysis* (New York 1966).

more or less available to anyone and the government put no restriction on the commercial nature of the British capital market. As new lands and new industries were opened up abroad, domestic saving was channelled to these foreign ventures even to the exclusion of what, in retrospect, were desirable investment opportunities at home. By 1875 it has been estimated that British investments abroad were of the order of £1,100 million, which by 1914 had risen to £4,000 million, and annual foreign investment was of the order of £200 million. The following table gives the relative importance of home and foreign capital formation.

TABLE 13

Trends in United Kingdom Capital Formation 1880–1914[a]

	Gross domestic fixed capital formation %	Net foreign investment %
1880–9	6·1	4·9
1890–9	6·9	3·2
1900–9	7·8	3·9
1905–14	6·0	6·9

[a] P. Deane and W. A. Cole *British Economic Growth 1688–1959* (Cambridge 1959), p. 308.

While it is impossible to be certain of the interrelationship between home and foreign investment, the authoritative opinion is that this huge foreign lending was, in the long run, undertaken at the expense of domestic capital formation,[2] which turned out to be inadequate to maintain the momentum of economic growth. The position was aggravated by the run-down of fixed assets in the First World War, so that by the end of the war there was a considerable backlog of domestic investment which had to be undertaken to modernize the economy.

The end of the war was followed by a short, sharp boom which ended in 1920/1, but which, for its short duration, did lead to a considerable spate of home investment, initially to replenish out-of-date plant, and later to create new plant to meet the growing demand generated by the boom. At first glance the figures for capital formation do not appear to bear this out as total capital formation in 1924–8, at 8·1 per cent of G.N.P., was far less than that in 1910–13 when it amounted to 11·2 per cent of G.N.P. The bare figures,

[2] A. K. Cairncross *Home and Foreign Investment 1870–1913* (Cambridge 1953), p. 187. For different views, however, see *The Export of Capital 1870–1914*, ed. A. R. Hall (1969).

however, conceal a highly significant change in the distribution of capital formation as between home and foreign investment.

TABLE 14

Net Domestic Capital Formation and Foreign Lending 1910–38[a]

	Net domestic capital formation		Net foreign lending		Total investment as % of G.N.P.
	£m.	% of G.N.P.	£m.	% of G.N.P.	
1910–23	65	3·0	180	8·2	11·2
1924–8	280	6·6	62	1·5	8·1
1929–33	186	4·6	– 5	–0·1	4·5
1934–8	347	7·7	–22	–0·5	7·7

[a] J. Jeffreys and D. Walters, 'National Income and Expenditure of the U.K. 1870–1952', *Income and Wealth Series VI*, p. 19.

Both as a percentage of G.N.P. and in absolute terms, net domestic capital formation in the period after World War I became by far the most important component of total net capital formation, and undoubtedly added to the long-run growth potential of the economy. Although in absolute terms consistently higher than in the pre-war years, net domestic capital formation did fluctuate markedly, rising to an early peak in 1921, declining in the depression which followed and then recovering against after 1924.

Around 1925 another significant break occurs in the pattern of capital investment. Previously much of the domestic capital formation was of a replacement kind. For instance in 1920–4 net capital formation never exceeded 23 per cent of G.N.P. After about 1925, however, net investment became substantially more important. Between 1925 and 1939 it ran at a normal level of about 30 per cent of the total, though continuing to show wide cyclical swings – falling as low as 11 per cent in the depression year of 1932. The remainder of the 1930s was a period of recovery from that nadir, though the heights reached at the end of the 1920s were not regained.

As we have seen, the warranted rate of investment can be defined as that which induces the full utilization of economic resources. As a measure of resource utilization we will take the figures for unemployment. Throughout the post-war period unemployment only very briefly fell below 10 per cent, rising as high as 20 per cent in some years in the 1930s. This would suggest that though there had been considerable improvement compared with pre-war years, net domestic investment was still inadequate. This was no doubt partly due to the peculiar nature of British economic development. Due in part to the substantial export of capital, Britain had failed to modernize her economy sufficiently to meet growing American and German competition at the turn of the century. Instead of investing in the so-called 'new industries' which turned out to be the basis of future economic development in other Western countries, British entrepreneurs had simply opened up new overseas markets for her traditional export products. Compared with other industrialized countries Britain's industrial structure in 1914 was very unbalanced, being far too dependent on the old staple industries, cotton, coal, iron and steel, on which her early prosperity was based. In the immediate post-war period this did not appear to be a drawback, for world demand for these products increased rapidly, so that in 1920 home investment, excluding dwellings, reached a maximum of £157m. However, as the boom soon passed, British industry was faced with a situation of excess capital in many industries, which decreased the profitability of further investment. Indeed, not until 1936 did the real level of investment exceed that of the 1920/1 boom. The reasons for this state of affairs were many and varied, but the immediate explanation was that already suggested: the international crisis affecting the staple trades and the relatively slow development of those industries that were the long-run growth points.

In the coal industry demand was maintained for a short time after the war, inducing an increase in capital formation up to 1923 (when it stood at £16·7m.). In 1925 and afterwards the secular forces in the international economy began to outweigh the short-term ones. Foreign markets declined, the uncompetitive position of the British industry became clear, German reparation payments virtually eliminated some British markets and the industry was faced with the problem of over-capacity. Although technical improvements increased the productivity of capital employed in the industry, the inducement to invest had been greatly reduced, and by 1928 capital formation had fallen to £3·8m. Investment in the industry did not again rise above £10m. throughout the inter-war period.

A similar tale can be told elsewhere. In the cotton industry investment reached a peak of £56m. in 1920, which was not reached again. Indeed, for most of the 1930s the cotton industry wrote off so much capital that it was a period of net dis-investment. In metal and metal-using industries a peak of £28·3m. was reached in 1920, and only attained again in 1934, after which there then occurred a fairly rapid increase up to 1937. Finally, in the iron and steel industry the maximum figure was reached in 1921/2 and was only reached again in 1934.[3]

These industries were major employers and the effect of this reduction in capital formation on the market for labour was unavoidable if the potential slack could not be taken up elsewhere in the economy. Growth in other sectors was in fact quite considerable; in electrical goods, artificial silk, motor cars, dyestuffs, etc., the annual increase in investment and in output was far greater than the average for British industry as a whole. However, the absolute size of these industries was so much smaller than that of the depressed industries, and the decline in the latter was so rapid that the unemployed resources just could not be absorbed.

Despite the fact that unemployment remained considerable, growth was high, and *per capita* income was rising rapidly.[4] This was partly due to normal expansionary forces within any mature economy. The growth of the new industries was extremely rapid, in part due to the backlog of unexploited technical advances. On the other hand the price of inputs was comparatively low. They were in elastic supply and there were thus few hindrances to this expansion of new industries.

If any constraint existed at all here, it would be on the demand side. But as we saw, although unemployment remained high it was very localized. In fact for those who were fortunate enough to be working, this was a period of substantial increase in real income. In part this was due to the fact that the price of domestically produced goods was low, but to a far greater extent it was due to contemporaneous changes in the external sector. The terms of trade in the period of the late twenties and early thirties moved decisively in favour of Britain.[5]

TABLE 15

Terms of Trade 1908–37[a]

	Export prices/Import prices 1913 = 100	Net terms of trade 1938 = 100
1908–13	97	143
1921–9	127	115
1930–7	138	103

[a] S. Pollard *The Development of the British Economy, 1914–1950* (1962), p. 189.

[3] For all this information, see C. Feinstein *Domestic Capital Formation 1920–1938* (1965), pp. 82, 109–15.

[4] See Chapter 1.

[5] See Chapter 6.

This improvement was essentially caused by falling prices of primary products, both absolutely and relative to manufactured goods. Since British imports were mainly of primary products the net effect was obvious and great.

Furthermore the high capital formation in the new industries was accompanied by an investment boom in the housing sector, associated with the twenty-year Kuznets cycle. Due to the First World War and the generally depressed conditions of the 1920s the normal cycle was interrupted, leading during the 1920s to a considerable shortage of houses which by 1930 was estimated at between 1·2 and 2 million. As conditions improved during the 1930s this backlog was taken up. In 1934/5, for instance, the number of houses completed amounted to 294,000, which represented a 100 per cent increase on 1932/3, and compares very favourably with a figure of 90,000 in 1921 (which was itself considered quite high). Although building only accounted for 6–7½ per cent of all insured workers in the country, 20 per cent of the increase in employment between 1932 and 1935 was attributable to the upsurge in the building industry, and if account is taken of associated sectors the figure is increased to 30 per cent. There were, of course, other stimuli to housebuilding in the period,[6] which was also associated with the boom in the demand for consumer durable goods.

It is certainly true that investment in the new consumer industries increased substantially throughout the inter-war period. At 1930 prices, investment in the motor vehicle increased from £3·8m. in 1920 to £5·2m. in 1931 and to £9·0m. in 1937, though there was a subsequent fall associated with the recession of 1938. (The expansion of the consumer durable industries contributed to the growth of some other manufacturers like glass, rubber and rayon.) There was an undoubted backlog of innovations which could be taken up in these sectors, which was largely due to the level of domestic investment in the immediately preceding decades. The economy had gone through a considerable process of modernization when the Second World War broke out.

During the war, investment was naturally enough concentrated on the war effort, even to the neglect of long-term peacetime development, and in many cases the capital stock was actually allowed to run down. Official estimates in fact show a net reduction in non-war capital formation from £214m. in 1938 to −£1,000 in 1940–5. This run-down was especially drastic in industries like coal and

[6] For a more detailed analysis of the importance of housebuilding, see Chapter 8.

transport which would obviously be vital for the post-war development of the economy. However, the need to meet the needs of a wartime economy led to considerable advances in industrial research and to the commercial development of new products and new techniques of control. Just as the first war advanced the development of glass, chemicals and aircraft, so the second provided electrical equipment, jet engines and computing and control equipment.

The two wars were alike in another way. After 1945 as after 1918, there was a sharp increase in the proportion of the economy's resources devoted to domestic capital formation. Investment as a percentage of G.N.P. increased from 3 per cent in 1910–13 to 6·6 per cent in 1924–8, and further increased from 7·7 per cent in 1934–8 to 15 per cent by the early 1950s. There was a further improvement in that net investment increased as a percentage of the whole, from 51 per cent of total capital formation in 1946 to 69 per cent in 1952, at which percentage it thereafter remained.

The role of investment in the growth process has been one of the central issues in the post-Harrod/Domar growth debate. Some economists have claimed that investment is a sufficient condition for economic growth, others that it is a necessary condition, and is important only in an indirect way through its impact on what has come to be called technical change. In the remainder of this chapter we shall review the arguments and the evidence on this rather confusing debate.

There is not complete agreement as to the cause of the increase in domestic capital formation. Some commentators have attributed it to the commitment of governments throughout the world to the maintenance of full employment requiring a high level of aggregate demand.[7] Other economists have queried this view. R. C. O. Matthews, with particular reference to the United Kingdom, claims that since the Second World War the direct effects of government budgetary policy have been deflationary in their impact.[8] Thus expansion must have originated from within the private sector, and in particular from a spectacular increase in private investment. This in turn might be held to be due to two factors:

(a) The Second World War, and indeed the whole period of war and depression since 1914, had created a flood of frustrated demands

[7] E.g. A. Maddison *Economic Growth in the West* (1964).

[8] R. C. O. Matthews, 'Why has Britain had full employment since the war?', *Economic Journal*, vol. 78, 1968. He does, however, agree that the government's commitment to keeping full employment may have affected the expectations and therefore the investment decisions of industrialists.

for consumer goods awaiting release. This pent-up demand induced private capital formation which in turn maintained the impetus to full employment and growth via the Keynesian multiplier process.

(b) The government's tax policy has had the effect of reducing the proportion of company income taken in tax (by the more generous treatment of profits), which has caused entrepreneurs to lower the rate at which they discount future profits.

The initial upsurge in private investment and the persistence of full employment no doubt interacted to keep investment and growth at an historically high level.

Despite the satisfactory performance of the economy in the post-war period, comparisons with other industrial economies showed Britain towards the bottom of the so-called growth league.[9] It was noted, besides, that the high growth countries were also countries which invested a high percentage of their national product.

TABLE 16

Investment and Growth in Some Selected European Countries 1953–61[a]

	Investment as percentage of G.N.P.	Rate of growth of G.N.P.
France	18·2	4·9%
Italy	20·8	6·2%
Germany	22·7	6·5%
United Kingdom	15·1	2·4%

[a] T. P. Hill, 'Growth and Investment According to International Comparisons', *Economic Journal*, vol. 74, 1964, p. 290.

The simple-minded conclusion was then drawn that high investment caused high growth, and that to increase her growth rate Britain would have to save a higher percentage of her national product. This argument was given intellectual respectability by the then dominant theory of economic growth – that of Harrod/Domar – which in its crude form emphasized the role of investment almost to the exclusion of other factors.

The interrelationship between the two variables, however, is obviously more complex than this, while the actual empirical evidence is far from clear. Although the high-growth countries were the countries which allocated a high percentage of G.N.P. to capital formation, the causal relationship has not been established. For it is suggested that high investment may well be as much a response to

[9] See Chapter 1.

as a cause of high growth, for instance through business expectations, etc. Professor Hill has analysed the relationship in a comparative manner and can only come to a qualified conclusion as to the interdependence of one or the other of the two variables. While he claims there to be 'no unique relationship' for the more developed countries as a whole, 'the rate of growth achieved by the larger European countries and the U.S.A. in recent years have in fact been quite strongly correlated with the share of the national product devoted to investment.'[10] For these countries the correlation coefficient is very high ($R^2 = 0{\cdot}96$). This correlation is exaggerated however by the large increase in the labour force which occurred in those same continental countries, requiring a substantial portion of investment as a concomitant factor input. If allowance is made for this fact, the high correlation previously found is reduced, R^2 being equal to 0·67,[11] though much of the reduction is caused by the bad fit of one country, that of France.

It is useful to isolate this particular group of countries for, with the addition of Japan, they generally provide the standard of reference by which the British performance is judged. If, however, the whole of Western Europe is analysed, including some of the comparatively underdeveloped countries and others of a small absolute size, the relationship is much less clear. The R^2 value falls to 0·49 and certain obvious anomalies appear. Norway, for instance, while investing almost 30 per cent of G.N.P. (more than any other considered) grew at the comparatively low rate of 3·2 per cent per annum. There may well be special forces at work in the case of Norway, but undoubtedly the strict relationship posited between investment and growth fails to hold. At the most we can say that high investment is necessary but not sufficient for growth.

On the other hand recent neo-classical theory plays down the direct impact of investment on the growth process. The Aggregate Production Function (A.P.F.) analysis makes the assumption of a Cobb–Douglas production function of the form $O = AL^aC^b$ where output (O) is a function of the increase in the supply of labour (L) and capital (C) and a residual item (A).[12] The exponents (a) and (b)

[10] T. P. Hill, 'Growth and Investment According to International Comparisons', *Economic Journal*, vol. 74, 1964, p. 287.

[11] Ibid., p. 292.

[12] For a more detailed analysis of the A.P.F. approach, see, for instance, E. F. Denison *The Sources of Economic Growth in the United States and the Alternatives Before Us* (New York 1967), and R. R. Nelson, 'Aggregate Production Functions and Medium Range Growth Projections', *American Economic Review*, vol. 54, 1964(2).

are usually given the values equivalent to the relative share of labour and capital in the national income of the country concerned (in industrial countries a rough 70:30 ratio.) (*a*) and (*b*) thus add up to one so that the model shows constant returns to scale. Conceptually at least, it is fairly straightforward to measure the contribution to economic growth of increases in the supply of capital and labour by simply multiplying the increase which has occurred in the given period by the appropriate exponent value. The difference between the figure thus produced and the actual growth observed in the period is said to be due to the residual factor or the (*A*) component in the model.

In the initial work done by Solow on growth in the U.S.A. between 1928 and 1955, investment was found to explain only 12 per cent of the growth which did occur, that is, investment does not appear to be very important. The Residual was thus left to account for 88 per cent of American growth,[13] and for want of a better alternative this dominant element of expansion was credited to technical improvement, that is, that contribution made to growth by increased efficiency in factor use as opposed to the simple increase in the supply of factors. The Residual has also, however, been called 'the extent of our ignorance'.[14]

This early analysis has since been considerably modified and the Residual item gradually broken down to its component parts. The amount left unexplained as technical change has been gradually reduced as growth was assigned to more specific causes. Nelson finds that, given the assumptions of the neo-classical model, technical change accounts for 66 per cent of American growth from 1929 to 1960.[15] For Norway Aukrust finds that it explains 54 per cent of observed growth between 1900 and 1955, while investment as such explains about 33 per cent.[16] The importance of investment *per se* is considerably reduced, though not abandoned; for instance Aukrust claims that, normally, the human factor alone will ensure a growth rate of 1·5 per cent whether investment is high or low.

To obtain similar results for Britain we must turn to the work of Denison.[17] As can be seen from Table 17 he estimates that the addition to capital accounted for only 21 per cent of the economic

[13] R. M. Solow, 'Technical Change and the Aggregate Production Function', *Review of Economics and Statistics*, vol. 39, 1957, p. 316.

[14] Nelson, op. cit., p. 578.

[15] Ibid., p. 579.

[16] O. Aukrust and J. Bjerke, 'Real Capital and Economic Growth in Norway', *Income and Wealth Series VIII* (1959).

[17] E. Denison *Why Growth Rates Differ* (Washington 1967).

growth achieved by Britain between 1950 and 1962. Within the general category of capital by far the most important single category was non-residential structures and equipment, which accounted for 86 per cent of the increase in the capital stock. The relative importance of investment in machinery and equipment is also borne out by other statistical work.[18]

TABLE 17

Sources and Percentage Distribution of Growth Rates in the U.K. 1950–62[a]

	Sources of growth		% distribution of growth rates	
	Total N.I.	N.I. per person employed	Total N.I.	N.I. per person employed
National income	2·29	1·63	100	100
Total factor input	1·11	0·45	47	20
Labour	0·60	0·10	25	6
Land	0·00	−0·02	0	−1
Capital	0·51	0·37	21	22
Dwellings	0·04	0·02	2	1
International assets	−0·05	−0·06	−2	−3
Non-residential structures	0·43	0·35	18	20
Inventories	0·09	0·06	4	3
Output per unit of input	1·18	1·18	53	74
Advances in knowledge	0·76	0·75	32	44
Economies of scale	0·36	0·36	15	21
Growth of national market	0·22	0·22	9	13

[a] E. Denison, op. cit., pp. 314–15.

As could be expected, the absolute contribution of investment to growth was smaller in Britain than in any other developed country apart from Belgium, though it turns out to be a big factor only in one country, Germany.

Though high investment does not of itself cause growth, it is easy to see why it should be associated with the residual item, technical change, which apparently does have such an important influence on the rate of economic growth.

On the one hand it is suggested that technical progress must be embodied in new capital and thus high growth and high rates of technical change 'necessitates high savings'. That is, the forces that activate the economy are closely interdependent and investment is of critical importance in realizing the potential of new knowledge.[19]

[18] Hill, op. cit., p. 297.

[19] R. M. Solow, 'Technical Progress, Capital Formation, and Economic Growth', *American Economic Review* Papers and Proceedings, vol. 52, 1962.

All new methods require investment outlays before they can be utilized irrespective of whether they are more mechanized or not.

In a country with a high rate of capital formation the average age of the capital stock should be lower than in a country where the capital stock grows only slowly. Thus the replacement element in gross capital formation would be lower and a higher percentage would be of a net kind which, presumably, would incorporate newer techniques and processes, etc. Thus the average productivity of the capital stock will be higher, the rate of return higher, and the contribution of investment to growth should also be greater.

New investment will not only reduce the average age of the capital stock, but it will also increase the flexibility of the economy. It is inevitable that in a mature economy technical change occurs at different rates in different industries, and as the pace of technical change varies so does the relative profitability of new investment. A high rate of technical change usually means high profitability of new investment, high inducement to invest, and a rapid writing-off of existing capital stock. To the extent that innovation is demand-determined,[20] the greater the flexibility of the economy to meet changes in demand, the greater the productivity of periods of production. An economy with a high rate of new capital formation is much more likely to be able to meet demand changes adequately and hence make the best use of the potentially available but uncommitted resources.

There may well be certain indirect relationships which will bring about a close correlation between the pace of technical change and the rate of growth of the capital stock. The main cause of the growth of real income is technical progress, and an increase of real income will generate demand for new investment. In this respect the causal relationship between investment and growth is the obverse of that normally posited.

Despite the A.P.F. analysis there is no statistical relationship between the rate of growth of capital and that of technical progress. Using the assumptions of the neo-classical model Aukrust has estimated the contribution made to economic growth by technical progress in a variety of countries over different periods of time. A comparison of the growth of capital stock in the same countries over the same periods gives the following results.

[20] See, e.g., J. Schmookler, 'The Determinants of Industrial Invention' in National Bureau of Economic Research *The Rate and Direction of Inventive Activity* (New York 1962).

TABLE 18

A Comparison of the Growth of Capital Stock and the Estimated Contribution of Technical Progress to Economic Growth 1949–54[a]

	Rate of growth of capital	Estimated contribution of technical progress
Belgium		
1 1949–54	2·4	2·5
2 1954–9	2·7	1·6
Canada		
3 1949–59	7·1	0·7
Netherlands		
4 1949–54	4·0	2·7
5 1954–9	5·5	1·6
Norway		
6 1949–59	4·4	2·3
Sweden		
7 1949–59	2·0	2·5
United Kingdom		
8 1949–59	3·1	1·2
France		
9 1949–54	2·9	3·8
10 1954–9	3·9	2·8
Italy		
11 1949–54	3·0	4·4
12 1954–9	3·4	4·1
West Germany		
13 1950–4	4·8	5·6
14 1954–9	6·9	3·5
Israel		
15 1952–8	11·8	3·9
Japan		
16 1950–8	10·6	3·0

[a] B. R. Williams, 'Investment and Technology in Growth', *Technology Investment and Growth* (1967), p. 115.

In diagrammatic form the lack of clear association becomes quite obvious.

There is no necessity for innovation in manufacturing industry to be accompanied by extra capital investment. The possibility of incorporating innovations through the normal process of capital replacement reduces the need to add to the capital stock, while, as Aukrust suggests, improvements in the quality of the labour input will add to growth without there being the need for any substantial investment at all.[21]

Whether in fact technical change is embodied or disembodied it

[21] Aukrust, op. cit., p. 6.

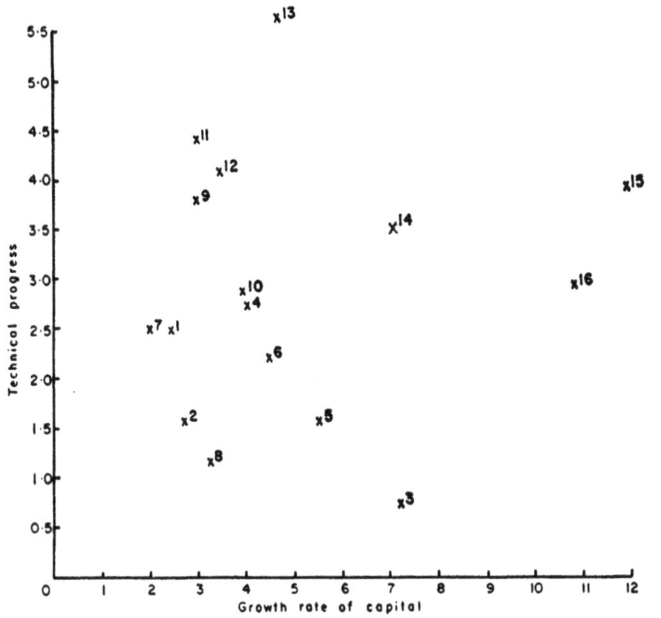

Growth Rate in Capital and Technical Progress for Selected Countries
SOURCE Williams, op. cit., p. 116.

obviously plays some, and possibly a very crucial, part in the process of growth. Ideally it would be very desirable to measure the role and determinants of technical change. At the moment this is impossible, but a substitute which may be more or less adequate is likely to be productivity change.

Strictly, productivity change should measure 'the relationship between changes in output and the quantities of the factors of production used in producing that output. . . . On the input side, therefore, [this is] the combined effects of changes in the quantity of labour and capital, use of raw materials, organization of production, etc.'.[22] In effect, due to the problems of measurement, productivity analysis usually refers to productivity of labour and even here there are certain conceptual and measurement difficulties.

However, such figures as are available indicate that throughout

[22] R. J. Nicolson and S. Gupta, 'Output and Productivity Changes in British Manufacturing Industry 1948–54', *Journal of the Royal Statistical Society*, series A, vol. 123, 1960, p. 440.

our period Britain achieved a fairly steady rate of productivity increase, though a rather slow one.

Average Rate of Productivity Increase[23]

	1924–35	1935–49	1945–55
All	2·2	1·3	3·2
Manufactures	2·0	2·0	3·1

For a somewhat later and slight different set of figures

Annual Percentage Increase in Productivity per Person Employed[24]

	1953–7	1957–61	1961–6
Industry	1·8	2·8	4·1
Rest of economy	1·8	2·0	2·6
G.D.P.	1·8	2·5	3·2

Throughout the period economists have found a marked association between output and productivity changes, the greatest increase in productivity occurring in those industries with the greatest increase in output, and the periods of most rapid growth of productivity being those when output has most increased. This also fits in with what we know from comparative studies, that those countries which experience high growth of G.N.P. are also those with a high productivity growth.

Again, however, this does not indicate causality. As with investment, high productivity growth may be a response to rapid change in G.N.P. The bulk of the evidence does seem to indicate, however, that the causal relationship is the other way, that growth in productivity has the effect of shifting the supply curve downward. If output growth was the independent variable, prices on the whole would be expected to rise, as firms operating at full capacity utilization push up short run costs. If, however, the causal factor was productivity change, the increased output should be accompanied by falling prices, the result of direct reductions or of increased sales. In fact for the British economy it has been shown that output and prices were negatively correlated at a significant level ($R^2 = 0{\cdot}55$),[25] which strongly suggests that the causal relationship runs from in-

[23] K. S. Lomax, 'Production and Productivity Movements in the United Kingdom Since 1900', *Journal of the Royal Statistical Society*, series A, vol. 122, 1959, p. 203.

[24] J. and A. M. Hackett *The British Economy* (1967), p. 118.

[25] Nicolson and Gupta, op. cit., p. 438.

creased productivity to growth. Thus if productivity could be increased, there is a strong presumption that growth would also increase.

It is suggested that one important determinant in the rate of technical change, productivity growth and in growth of G.N.P. may be the amount of resources devoted to what has now come to be called Research and Development. The implication is very often that the greater the amount spent on R. & D., *ceteris paribus*, the higher will be the rate of growth. In fact, expenditure on R. & D. in Britain is extremely high, being about £800 million in 1963/4, 2·3 per cent of G.N.P.

The relationship between R. & D. expenditures and growth is a very tenuous one, however, and there is no statistical evidence of any causality, as Table 19 shows.

TABLE 19

Economic Growth and R. & D. Expenditures 1950–64[a]

	Absolute amount* $ million	% of G.N.P.*	Growth of real national income
Japan	646	1·4	8·7
Germany	1,110	1·4	7·1
Italy	238	0·6	5·6
France	958	1·6	4·9
U.S.A.	18,117	3·4	3·5
U.K.	1,917	2·3	2·6

* For period 1963/4

[a] Organization for European Co-operation and Development, 'The Overall Level and Structure of R. & D. Efforts in O.E.C.D. Member Countries' (O.E.C.D.), Table 2.

A straightforward comparison of this kind may fail to isolate the indirect impact of the R. & D. effort on economic growth. It is, for instance, highly probable that the importance of the education sector in the growth process which is elsewhere noted is partly explained by R. & D. expenditures, in that highly trained technical personnel can only fully exploit their particular expertise if associated and highly specialized factor inputs are readily available.

On the other hand there is no reason to suppose that the British growth potential would be increased by adding to the amount spend on R. & D. Indeed, given the opportunity cost involved, a transfer of scientific resources may well have an inhibiting effect on growth.

Given the prohibitive cost of a comprehensive R. & D. effort, there may well be economies to be reaped by a redistribution of scientific resources. In Great Britain about 40 per cent of the total R. & D. expenditure is concentrated in the defence sector and over 30 per cent in a single industry, the aircraft industry. There may well be spin-offs to the rest of the economy, but this must be considered an extremely inefficient method of providing new techniques and new materials for the rest of the economy. Defence research is getting increasingly sophisticated and the value of these external effects must be very small for those sectors engaged in the more mundane process of manufacturing. For instance in the U.S.A. from 1951 to 1965 (the only figures readily available) while 50 per cent of company R. & D. was defence financed, only 4 per cent of all patents taken out came from these contracts. There is no reason to suppose that the British figures would be significantly different.

A second source of misallocation is the apparently excessive concentration on scientists with consequent shortages of applied engineers. Inventions are only economically useful to the extent that they can be adapted, absorbed and processed into the economic system, which is partly a function of the supply of qualified engineers. As Table 20 shows, Britain appears to be peculiarly badly off in this respect.

TABLE 20

Percentage Distribution of Engineers and Scientists in Industry 1959[a]

	Engineers	Natural scientists	% of total scientists and engineers in industry as % of all scientists and engineers
U.K.	54	43	42
U.S.A.	71	25	74
Belgium	77	14	54
France	67	21	52
Netherlands	80	12	n.a.

[a] M. Peck and R. Nelson *Technology, Economic Growth and Public Policy* (Washington 1967), p. 451.

Not only is there a higher concentration of natural scientists and a lower percentage of engineers than in other countries, but a far lower proportion (of both) work in the industrial sector where the work is likely to be most fruitful in contributing to economic growth. In this sense it can be said that there is too much research and too little development, for 'it is not true that the locus of basic research determines the locus of innovation'.[26]

This is not to say that Britain should give up pure research, but she should concentrate her effort in R. & D. on those sectors where she has the greatest comparative advantage. At the moment this appears to be in those sectors where the scientific content of final production is high. This specialization should eventually lead to a more formal co-operation with other countries in a complementary situation to her, such as France and Germany for instance.

There seems little doubt that the increase in the growth of the British economy was closely associated with an increase in both gross and net capital formation. The precise relationship, however, is still somewhat unclear. The debate continues as to whether investment has a direct and immediate impact on growth, or whether the effect is more diffused, operating indirectly via technical progress. We are still not sure whether investment is sufficient or merely necessary, for growth.

ADDITIONAL READING

A. K. CAIRNCROSS *Home and Foreign Investment, 1870–1913* (Cambridge 1963); *Factors in Economic Development* (1962)

R. E. CAVES *Britain's Economic Prospects* (Washington 1968)

E. DENISON *Why Growth Rates Differ* (Washington 1967)

C. FEINSTEIN *Domestic Capital Formation, 1920–38* (1962)

T. P. HILL 'Growth and Investment According to International Comparisons' (*Economic Journal*, vol. 74, 1964)

K. B. PAVITT AND S. WALD *The Conditions for Success in Technological Innovation* (Paris O.E.C.D. 1971)

W. SALTER *Productivity and Technical Change* (1960)

[26] H. Hufbauer *Synthetic Materials and the Theory of International Trade* (1966), p. 86.

CHAPTER 4

Some Aspects of Management

The view that the supply of managerial talent is a contributory factor in economic growth rests upon common sense rather than theoretical or empirical demonstration. Marginalist economic theory, as applied to the subject of the firm, has kept to a high level of abstraction: it has been called, epigrammatically, 'a fascinating paradox that the received theory of the firm, by and large, assumes that the firm does not exist'.[1] The motive and behaviour which this theory ascribes to managers, in other words, are admittedly unrealistic. Even if they were more true to life, however, it would still be difficult to establish the nature of the connection between efficient management in the setting of the individual firm and the performance of the economy as a whole – or the extent to which entrepreneurs in general could exercise freedom of choice. Clearly there are areas in which industrialists can and do enjoy significant powers of decision and discretion, especially in the field of investment. There is evidence that industrialists accept higher or lower rates of return over longer or shorter periods, and vary the profit retention ratio (the proportion of net earnings ploughed back as investment). They have also, of course, wide scope for initiative in such matters as the organization of the factory and the management of its 'human relations'. But it is impossible to measure the difference made to output or productivity by the quality of one company's directorate in relation to another's; still more so to assess the total effect of managerial talent or enterprise on the size of the 'residual'. Managers, like philosophers, are parasitic upon other disciplines, and the element of their work for which they are peculiarly responsible cannot be separated out.

This chapter takes as a starting point, therefore, what is an apparently obvious, but nonetheless fairly intuitive assumption: that 'the growth of the firm is greatly influenced by the personal characteristics and attitudes of management. Hence greater progress

[1] H. B. Thorelli *The Political Economy of the Firm*, quoted in F. Machlup, 'Theories of the Firm: Marginalist, Behavioural, Managerial' (*American Economic Review*, vol. 57, 1967).

in the firm, and in the economy, is attainable by an improved social selection of management and by the development of those characteristics of management which make for success in business'.[2] It must be admitted, however, that even the first part of this hypothesis is not above question. The study of the medium-term profit records of selected manufacturing firms by Rayner and Little yielded a pattern of individual growth rates which appeared largely random, and led them to pose the question, was there such a thing as good management?[3] At the very least it seems difficult for any firm to perform *consistently* well – to avoid relaxing its efforts, developing 'organizational slack', or encountering the classic problems of hypertrophy attendant upon continuous growth.[4] And it may be almost as uncommon for any enterprise to perform consistently badly, without suffering absorption; there are, at any rate, several well-established routes by which an unprogressive firm can rehabilitate itself. Thus it seems likely that the historian of management is confronted with an immensely fluid situation. The capacity of any given management can be expected to vary over time with the circumstances of its own industry (the growth of demand, the rapidity of technical change and so forth) and with the performance of competing firms. Generalizations about the typical condition of industrial executives and administrators are bound to be impressionistic, and open to manifold qualifications and exceptions.

In face of these uncertainties, however, we may locate two firmer reference points. Firstly, most economists would find no difficulty in agreeing upon a set of criteria by which managerial efficiency could be judged (and some at least of which would be accepted by industrialists).[5] Secondly, there is good evidence to hold that firms exhibiting the characteristics of efficiency do enjoy, in relation to their own trade or industry, a satisfactory rate of growth and profit-

[2] T. Barna, 'Investment and Growth Policies in British Industrial Firms' (N.I.E.S.R. Occas. Paper 20, Cambridge 1962), p. 59.

[3] A. C. Rayner and I. M. D. Little *Higgledy Piggledy Growth Again* (Oxford 1966).

[4] Whether the limitations of management act as a constraint on growth once a firm has reached a given size is a vexed theoretical question: see for example E. A. G. Robinson *The Structure of Competitive Industry* (1958 edn), pp. 46–8; P. W. S. Andrews *Manufacturing Business* (1949), pp. 130–44. In practice, there would seem no doubt that at least some firms experience a problem of this kind.

[5] C. F. Carter and B. R. Williams *Industry and Technical Progress* (1957), pp. 178–83; P.E.P. *Thrusters and Sleepers* (1965). There is more agreement, however, on what constitutes desirable attitudes in management, than on rules of behaviour and organization. See Joan Woodward *Industrial Organization: Theory and Practice* (1965), pp. 68–72, 241–57.

ability – though not necessarily one closely correlated to that of other similar firms. Conversely, establishments which are clearly 'inefficient' by these standards might enjoy years of good fortune, but will tend to do worse than their rivals over a period of time.

Even granted this consensus, however, the problems confronting the historian of twentieth-century management are all but insuperable. The task of applying common standards of efficiency to a class of industrialists so diverse in character and subject to such different circumstances is itself formidable enough. To relate such a judgement on the capacity of British industrialists to the performance of the national economy is, as has been seen, pretty well impossible. The conclusion to this chapter cannot be stated more specifically than this: that the shortcomings prevalent among the industrial leadership of the nation have played some part, however indeterminate, in curtailing the rate of national economic growth.

What was the extent and nature of these shortcomings? In so far as professional economists in the past have given opinions on their own generation of businessmen, their views were understandably inconsistent. We may begin, perhaps, with Marshall's celebrated description of the contrast between the innovating entrepreneur typical of the first industrial revolution and his filial successors:[6]

> strong self-reliant energy lost some of its importance relatively to a sedulous care for detail; . . . the son of a manufacturer profited by tradition as to things, methods and persons handed down to his father and a youth who rose from the ranks into business had to overcome more difficulties on his way than during times of revolutionary change.

This presumption, of the debilitating effects of the hereditary principle in industry, though it originated during the Great Depression, remained influential in the period of high unemployment between the wars.[7]

As against this, we may cite the view of Keynes (among others), that the progress of industry and the steady growth in the size of the firm gave birth to a new and more professional kind of management:

[6] A. Marshall *Industry and Trade* (1919), pp. 358–9; quoted in C. Erickson *British Industrialists: Steel and Hosiery* (Cambridge 1959), p. 10. For other Marshallian dicta on the same theme, see A. L. Levine *Retardation in the British Economy, 1870–1914* (1967), p. 58.

[7] See, for example, The Liberal Party *Britain's Industrial Future* (1928), pp. 127–8.

> The trend of Joint Stock Institutions, when they have reached a certain age and size, [is] to approximate more to the status of public corporations rather than that of individualistic private enterprise. The shareholders are almost entirely dissociated from the management, with the result that the direct personal interest of the latter in the making of great profit becomes quite secondary. When this stage is reached, the general stability and reputation of the institution are more considered by the management than the maximum of profit for the shareholders. The shareholders must be satisfied by conventionally adequate dividends; but once this is secured, the direct interest of the management often consists in avoiding criticism from the public and from the customers of the concern. . . . Many big institutions . . . are, as time goes on, socializing themselves.[8]

In this statement we have an early, if overstated, testimony to the rise of an industrialist class divorced from ownership and the evolution of a distinctive form of 'managerial' capitalism. The significance of these changes has been much studied from the First World War on.[9] They were generally supposed to promote industrial progress, both because of the increasing specialization associated with managerial forms of organization – the cultivation of new areas of business expertise – and because management was held to be less concerned by profits in themselves than by the growth and security of the firm.

Ever since the late nineteenth century, therefore, the condition of management has been the subject of contrasting opinions; symptoms were seen, both of diminishing energy and adventurousness, and of increasing sophistication and social awareness. These two states were not incompatible, however; indeed, it is highly probable

[8] J. M. Keynes *The End of Laissez-Faire* (1927), pp. 42–3. For the expression of a similar view by an industrialist, see Sir Alfred Mond, 'Modern Industrial Problems' (*Industry and Politics*, 1927, p. 38):

> The terms 'employer' and 'employed', 'master' and 'man', are inapplicable to our modern industrial conditions. Few men are at the same time capitalists, who own the business, and its managers. . . . Management is nowadays, and always has been, one of the most vital functions in an industrial concern. Capital is necessary, labour is necessary, but the two are sterile unless you have competent management.

[9] J. Child *British Management Thought* (1969); ed. A. Tillett, T. Kempner and G. Wills *Management Thinkers* (1970); Theo Nichols *Ownership, Control and Ideology* (1969). The philosophy of 'scientific management' developed earlier in the U.S.A. For this see L. H. Jenks, 'Early Phases of the Management Movement' (*Administrative Science Quarterly*, 5, 1960/1).

that they coexisted. The evidence for continued managerial proficiency was to be found simply in the successful adaptation of firms to large-scale business operations,[10] the rapidity, in some industries, of technical change, and the improvement, patchy though it was, of domestic investment and productivity. At any rate these developments could not take place without managers and industrialists taking appropriate decisions at certain times. The evidence for the deficiencies of management is more diffuse, and requires more careful consideration.

In the first place, it can be pointed out that ever since 1918 the competence of Britain's industrial leaders has been the subject of fairly persistent criticism, much of it well-informed and disinterested. Even before the First World War, the views of Marshall had been echoed by others, who found in the failure of late-Victorian Britain to hold her own against foreign competition signs of the inadequate direction of her industries. The war itself exposed the backwardness of the heavy industries, and especially the slowness with which they had adopted standardization and mass production.[11] During the depression of the 1920s the Balfour Committee reported of its investigation into the conduct of the exporting industries,[12]

> we have repeatedly been led to the conclusion that at present one of the most serious obstacles to progress is the defective sympathy on the part of persons holding responsible positions in industry and trading enterprises with new ideas and propositions which involve a radical change of customary practice or a new orientation of outlook.

The coal industry was heavily criticized for the inefficiency of its management, by two Royal Commissions in 1919 and 1926; and similarly authoritative strictures were levelled against the cotton industry, pottery, iron and steel, road haulage and others.[13]

[10] But see below, pp. 80–1.

[11] D. H. Aldcroft, 'The Performance of the British Machine-Tool Industry in the Interwar Years' (*Bus. Hist. Rev.*, 40, 1966); L. Urwick and E. F. L. Brech *The Making of Scientific Management* (1946), vol. ii, p. 91; A. S. Milward *The Economic Effects of the Two World Wars on Britain* (1970), pp. 33–4. The report of the Engineering Trades Committee of the Board of Trade, for instance, said (in 1917) that it had been 'much impressed . . . by the very large number of relatively small firms that exist – each with a separate organization, separate establishment charges, separate buying and selling arrangements, and each producing a multiplicity of articles' (quoted in P. Sargant Florence *The Logic of British and American Industry* (1953)), p. 83.

[12] Committee on Industry and Trade *Final Report* 1929, pp. 245–6.

[13] The 1919 (Sankey) Reports, Cmds. 359 and 360; the 1926 (Samuel) Report, on

Since the Second World War, although the public standing of management has improved, it has still met with frequent criticism. Some industries were still very incompletely 'rationalized' even in the 1950s; the British Productivity Council reported on the machine tool trades in 1953, for example, that 'firms are generally independent, individualistic, and to a large extent privately owned.... Each firm is generally too jealous of its individuality and independence to pay much more than lip service to any idea of industry-wide standardization and rationalization, to the great detriment of productivity and exasperation of the consumer.'[14] This was a reiteration of charges made a generation before.[15] In the docks industry, too, the Devlin Report of 1965 condemned the casual system of labour hiring, on grounds not unlike those cited by the Shaw Inquiry forty-five years earlier.[16] Both the N.E.D.C. and the Prices and Incomes Board issued reports suggesting, directly or indirectly, that many individual firms, and large sections of some industries, were inured to backwardness and resistant to change.[17]

What underlies this persistent current of criticism? One probable factor is the inability or unwillingness of the industrial elite in the period since 1918 to introduce new talent into their circle. This difficulty of promotion is partly a reflection of the diminishing number of business enterprises, and the growing problems, which Marshall first noticed, in the way of starting new companies (see Table 21). But it is also an indication of the selectiveness, social and educational, of the managerial recruitment system. In the two industries of steel and hosiery, studied by Dr Erickson, the higher ranks of the industrial hierarchy were dominated, from the 1920s to the 1950s, by the sons of middle-class fathers; only since the Second World War have men from lower social origins entered such jobs in significant numbers, and they remained a small pro-

the Coal Mining industry; the (Baillie) Committee on the Road Haulage Industry, Cmd. 5440, 1937; Balfour Committee on Industry and Trade, *Factors in Industrial and Commercial Efficiency* (1927), *Survey of the Textile Industries* (1928), *Survey of the Metal Industries* (1928). See also J. R. Jones *et al. Britain in Depression* (1933); I. Thomas, 'The Coal Mines Reorganization Commission', in W. Robson (ed.) *Public Enterprise* (1937).

[14] Aldcroft, op. cit.

[15] Balfour Committee *Factors in Industrial and Commercial Efficiency* (1927), pp. 295–8.

[16] Court of Inquiry into Wages and Conditions of Dock labour, Cmd. 936, 1920.

[17] N.E.D.C. *Conditions Favourable to Faster Growth* (1963), paras. 18, 27, 29; G. Radice *Low Pay*.

portion.[18] The growth of larger public companies has made little impression on this exclusiveness, for although it has somewhat reduced the frequency of hereditary succession among directors it has not led to any larger intake of men from a white-collar or working-class background. It seems unlikely that the picture is much different in other industries, or has altered radically since the mid-1950s.[19]

TABLE 21

Number of Joint Stock Companies in G.B., 1914–60

	Public	Private
1914	14,270	48,492
1921	12,923	67,071
1939	14,500	145,000
1960	10,900	368,000

SOURCES Balfour Committee *Factors in Industrial and Commercial Efficiency*; Dunning and Thomas *British Industry.*

The relative difficulty of newcomers in gaining access to the industrial elite did not, of course, mean that outstanding individual entrepreneurs were absent from the scene in this period. The inter-war years witnessed many of the achievements of such men as Lords Leverhulme and Nuffield, Hans Renold, Cecil Pilkington, and Samuel Courtauld – though their firms were mostly established before the First World War. The trend towards large-scale companies, however, appears to have made it difficult for such highly idiosyncratic talents to survive. The problems of running such giant organizations were demonstrated, in different ways, both by Unilever and I.C.I. The former combine displayed the paradoxical character of an enterprise dependent on a single, dominating head, yet with an administrative machine so complicated that three sales departments were required to sell its products. I.C.I., having begun as a merger with high concentration of power in 1926, found it necessary to introduce a measure of decentralization by 1930. Vast enterprises of

[18] The percentage of steel manufacturers who were sons of businessmen fell from 55 to 34 between 1905–25 and 1953, those who were sons of middle-class fathers from 87 to 62. In hosiery, the proportion of middle-class executives *increased* between the 1930s and the 1950s. See C. Erickson, op. cit., pp. 12, 103–4.

[19] In 1966 *The Director* reported that 63 per cent of a sample of industrial directors were sons of businessmen, and 56 per cent obtained their first job through family or social contacts, or in a family firm ('The Director Observed', April 1966).

this kind were obviously difficult to subject to close personal control, and were unlikely to reproduce the heroic figures who created them. If modern corporations exhibit personalities, they are normally collective ones.

A second, though perhaps related, ground for questioning the competence of higher management in this period is its want of professional and educational qualifications. Management training has been slow to develop in Great Britain. A handful of universities provided degrees or diploma courses in commerce and business between the wars, although these were chiefly intended for accountants.[20] Technical education was more readily available, but rarely offered in a form appropriate for prospective managers. A number of professional institutes were established immediately before or after the First World War – the Institute of Industrial Administration, the Institute of Labour Management and the Institute of Works Managers – intended to strengthen the identity and raise the standards of the occupation. They attracted few members, however, and exerted little practical influence in industry. Britain was one of the few Western countries to remain aloof from the international influence of 'managerial' ideology and organizations in the inter-war years.

This state of affairs has changed, though again only slowly, since the second war.[21] The representativeness of management bodies has increased, especially since the merger of the British Institute of Management and the Institute of Industrial Administration in 1951. The idea of professional training has gained ground through the business schools and diplomas set up since 1961. But in 1966 still only 21 per cent of industrial directors had received some formal training in management, whilst between 50 and 60 per cent lacked any kind of advanced education.[22] Moreover the idea of management as a profession, admission to which is dependent on approved qualifications and specialized knowledge, is still apparently accepted by only a small minority of its practitioners.

[20] Urwick and Brech, op. cit., ii, pp. 141–3. The most important were Manchester, Birmingham and L.S.E.

[21] Cf. Woodward, op. cit., p. 254: 'Ten years [from the early 1950s to the early 1960s] saw the final emergence of management as a social institution in this country: a group of people bound together by a common ideology or system of beliefs.' But she adds that these beliefs were not based on objective and rational inquiry.

[22] Nichols, op. cit., pp. 80–3. The proportion with technical qualifications had increased since the 1930s, however: see D. P. Barritt, 'The Stated Qualifications of Directors of Larger Public Companies' (*J. Ind. Econs.*, 5, 1956–7). These figures apply to directors only; for the educational experience of managers, see G. H. Copeman *Managers*, and Acton Society Trust *Management Succession*.

To judge the efficiency of industrial management wholly by reference to its educational experience would, of course, be unfair. Other evidence suggests greater progressiveness and receptivity to change. There is little doubt, for instance, that most firms have displayed a consistent sophistication in financial matters since 1918. The impact of professional accountancy had been felt since the late nineteenth century. And a similar effect was produced, between the wars, by the growing involvement of banks and finance houses in industry. By the post-war period the largest British firms made it a rule to have some representative of banking on their boards. There is no doubt, too, that a growing proportion of industrialists had had *experience* of management (whether or not they have been trained) before reaching high office in their firm. The sharp distinction between the functions of director and executive, still maintained in the 1920s, has broken down, and a good part of that class of 'parasitical', inactive directors of those years, about which Stanley Baldwin complained, has disappeared.[23]

It can also be shown that, independently in part of their own technical training, industrialists have paid increasing attention to the subject of research and development. Originally this interest was prompted by the government, which during and after the First World War helped to finance co-operative industrial research associations. Twenty-one bodies of this kind were set up before 1921, although only sixteen survived to 1927. From the 1930s, industry itself took up the running, spurred on now, perhaps, by the example of American subsidiaries established in Britain following the imposition of a general tariff. Those private firms belonging to the F.B.I. spent an estimated £1,680,000 on research and development in 1930, and £5,189,000 by 1938 (by when another £450,000 or so was disbursed by the research associations). The increase in this expenditure since the Second World War, however, has been much more spectacular. In 1958/9 private industry was devoting about £134m. to this item, excluding official assistance; by 1964/5 this had risen to an estimated £327·8m. The total national expenditure on research in recent years, as a proportion of national income, compared well with that of almost all other Western industrial countries.[24]

[23] Erickson, op. cit., pp. 188, 195–7. The number of industrialists in steel who began their careers as 'administrators' increased from 30 per cent of the total in 1905–25 to 49 per cent in 1953; of hosiers, from 13 per cent in 1900 to 31 per cent in 1952. Ibid., pp. 51, 123.

[24] O.E.C.D., *The Overall Level and Structure of R. & D. efforts in O.E.C.D. member countries* (Paris 1967). For a fuller discussion of this topic, see above, Chapter 3.

This discussion of the history of management is clearly very incomplete, based only on that evidence which is easily obtainable and risking only those judgements which seem most representative. There remain many other fields of managerial practice, of course (apart from the problem of labour relations which is discussed below) which have been passed over: the whole question of investment planning, the internal organization of firms, the arrangement of production processes, the conduct of marketing, and so on. On these subjects, generalization is almost impossible, except in relation to the individual firm or industry. One other facet of industrial organization has, however, received more attention from economists: the measurement of industrial concentration. The growth in size of firms and the degree of market control they exercise at least provide a context of managerial activity in this period, and perhaps may cast some light on its standard of efficiency. This aspect of economic development is thus worth some consideration.

Concentration is conventionally measured in terms of the share in employment or output of the three largest firms in an industry.[25] Changes in the level of market concentration result principally from two factors.[26] The first is the tendency of individual firms to grow bigger: this must lead to increased concentration in face of a declining or stagnant market, and may do so in an expanding market if the optimum size of plants or firms increases more rapidly than the rate of demand for their products. The second contributory factor is the inclination of firms, on reaching a given size, to diversify their products. In principle this might as well lead to a reduction in concentration as to a rise; but the fact that multiproduct firms usually employ large resources in all their spheres of activity, and that their favourite methods of extending their range of output is by amalgamation or takeover, give them a significant part in the process of intensifying oligopoly.

The evidence concerning concentration in British industry since 1935 is presented in Table 22. No adequate figures exist for the period before the 1935 census of production, but there is sufficient reason to argue that the movement towards consolidation in larger units began well before then. Certainly some celebrated (or notorious) examples of trusts and combines dated from the late nineteenth

[25] For a full discussion of alternative approaches, see M. A. Utton *Industrial Concentration* (1970), chap. III.

[26] 'Market concentration' refers to concentration in a particular trade or industry. Overall concentration changes, of course, with the expansion or contraction of different industries subject to varying degrees of monopoly.

century, even though the conditions of free trade, competitive markets and business traditions were then antithetical to such developments. Concentration was carried further in some sectors under the impact of the First World War, following which government action was briefly taken to investigate some quasi-monopoly concerns.[27] Growth in the mean size of plants, under the influence especially of technological factors, was continuous throughout this period – as it had been, indeed, throughout the whole process of industrialization.

TABLE 22

Distribution of Enterprises by Size, 1935 and 1963

Enterprises of	Number of enterprises 1935	Number of enterprises 1963	Total number of employees (thousands) 1935	Total number of employees (thousands) 1963
50,000+employees	2	10	141	728
20,000–49,999	8	28	312	941
10,000–19,999	21	60	284	824
5,000–9,999	70	112	710	799
1,000–4,999	858	767	1,529	1,741
100–999	10,992	6,563	2,872	1,787
25–99	23,606	11,551	1,148	606
less than 25	17,609*	45,276	304*	438

* Enterprises of 11–24 employees. There were altogether 149,947 enterprises of 1–24 employees in 1935 (*British Labour Statistics, 1886–1968*, footnote to Table 206).

SOURCES Leak and Maizels *J.R.S.S.* 108, 1945; Board of Trade *Census of Production 1963* vol. 132, table 13.

Between 1935 and the census of production in 1951 the level of industrial concentration advanced imperceptibly, and may actually have diminished. In the 1950s and 1960s, however, there has been a notable revival of the trend, resulting chiefly from the frequency of mergers and takeovers in the manufacturing sector. The outcome was in part to unify the control of those industries, like aircraft construction and the manufacture of telephone apparatus, which had been least subject to monopoly tendencies earlier; but also to increase the concentration ratio of industries like chemicals, motor

[27] Through the Committee on Trusts in 1918, and the standing committees under the Profiteering Act of 1919. For the simultaneous connivance of the courts in monopolistic practices, however, see Sir David Cairns, 'Monopolies and Restrictive Practices', in M. Ginsberg (ed.) *Law and Opinion in the Twentieth Century* (1955).

vehicles and tobacco, which had already reached a state of relatively high integration. By the end of the 1960s the 100 largest firms probably controlled over 60 per cent of the net assets in manufacturing industry. Only a few trades, catering for specialist markets and producing variegated commodities – like textiles and machine tools – had held back from the movement towards amalgamation.

In theory, it has been suggested, the consolidation of industry into fewer and large units is beneficial to internal efficiency and to potential growth of output. Gains can be made in the form of bulk transactions, massed reserves (stocks held in common between several departments or establishments) and specialization of labour or management.[28] However, the economic literature on the subject reveals that in practice the reasons for and objectives of increased concentration, especially when achieved by means of mergers, are by no means synonymous with greater efficiency and higher growth. It is not possible, in other words, to explain the progress of concentration as simply a reflection of the desire of management to maximize productivity; or, as Evely and Little put it, 'a considerable part of the variation in concentration is, and always will be, inexplicable in terms of easily measurable economic facts'.[29] Other, more elusive, motives may prompt industrialists to enlarge their enterprises or to promote amalgamations: a desire to curtail competition, to enhance prestige or security, even to avert the chance of themselves being the victims of a takeover. Whilst the weight of these considerations is difficult to assess, two points are clear: firstly, the size of many very large companies has far exceeded the minimum scale required for efficient technical or financial operation – that is, the increases in concentration, especially at the beginning and end of this period, are not accompanied by any equivalent increase in the optimal size of firm in the industries concerned. Secondly, it is implausible to attribute more than a small part of the lag of Britain's rate of growth of productivity behind that of other countries to differences in the size of plant (or *a fortiori*, size of firms). The benefits of very large-scale production in recent years, though they probably exist, appear to have been more fully exploited in Germany, for instance, than in the United Kingdom. It would seem, too, that at least part of this superiority is derived, in one way or another, from the quality of management – that the way to the success or

[28] For a full explanation of these principles of organization, see P. S. Florence *The Logic of British and American Industry* (1953), pp. 49–51.

[29] R. Evely and I. Little *Concentration in British Industry* (Cambridge 1960), pp. 174–5.

failure of mergers, in fact, lies here. In the British context the evidence of concentration, like the other evidence that has been considered, leads to a verdict on managerial performance which is reserved and ambiguous, but certainly not completely favourable.

Industrial Relations

Collective bargaining with labour has been, for most of the period since 1918, a fairly minor interest of industrial management. Negotiations with trade unions have been relinquished to employers' associations at national or district level, and such bargaining as has taken place at shopfloor level has been left to junior members of the managerial hierarchy. Where firms have employed specialist personnel officers to take charge of labour relations, their authority and position in the managerial hierarchy have often been uncertain and in practice inconsequential.

This neglect of labour management can be explained in various ways. Much can be attributed to tradition and force of habit. Industrial relations had never been regarded as a major concern of industrialists before 1914; and such initiatives as were taken were the responsibility of employers' federations rather than individual companies. Although necessarily the subject assumed more importance after the First World War, the focus of responsibility did not change. Secondly, in the twentieth century as in the nineteenth, employers tended to resent the encroachment of trade unions upon their own 'prerogatives'. Even when it became desirable or expedient to negotiate with unions on issues of wages and hours, managers and directors continued to feel it undesirable that labour organizations should trespass upon any other fields of their activity. Thirdly, the great majority of managers certainly failed to appreciate how far labour productivity and efficiency could be influenced by collective bargaining. It was assumed that by keeping trade unions weak and at arm's length, companies would secure employees more tractable and co-operative. Only gradually did it come to appear that this might well be the reverse of the truth.

Most employers, politicians and economists failed to understand (and many still do not) that labour combination has various and subtle forms. There are two direct means by which employees can interrupt or curtail industrial production: strike action and restrictive labour practices.[30] Neither of these weapons, however, is the peculiar

[30] Production is also limited by absenteeism, sickness and industrial accidents, all of which are influenced (though to an unknown degree) by the attitudes of workers, and are thus susceptible to reduction by managerial policies (H. A.

possession of trade unions. Although in the inter-war years most stoppages were official, since 1945 the vast bulk of industrial disputes have begun, and often ended, without the knowledge or approval of the organization whose members were involved. And restrictive practices – defined as 'arrangement[s] under which labour is not used efficiently and which [are] not justifiable on social grounds'[31] – are neither created nor in many cases enforced by union action. Thus even in the 1930s one inquiry in this area could conclude: 'The evidence presented inclines us to the view that restrictive stipulations and practices are at least as common where the organizations of workers and employers are feeble or in a bad way as where they are strong and effective.'[32] Other aspects of working-class behaviour which indirectly hamper industrial efficiency are even less attributable to union policy. Systematic overtime has become endemic since 1918, and especially since 1945, despite the fact that almost every major union makes its abolition a stated objective. Antiquated and often meaningless wage differentials have survived in practice, even though union officials have recurrently sought to reduce or eliminate them by claiming flat-rate increases. All these inconsistencies in the labour market testify to the importance and inherent conservatism of the work group, as distinct from the trade union. This primary social group, determining the wage-earners' behaviour at the place of work, has exercised a constant and powerful influence on the pattern of industrial relations.

Management, then, in its conduct of industrial relations since 1918, has been preoccupied until recently with formal rather than informal institutions, trade unions rather than work groups, national negotiations rather than company ones. To a large extent, therefore, in tackling the problems of labour inefficiency, it has been concerned with the symptoms rather than the disease. Why its perspective was for long so unrevealing – and why it has changed in recent years – will become clear if we look briefly at the historical development of industrial relations since 1918.

It was in the years following the First World War that the framework of national bargaining was established in Britain, albeit its construction was by no means completed. The official Committee

Turner *Is Britain really Strike-Prone?* (Cambridge, D.A.E. Occasional Paper 20, 1969), p. 34; J. E. T. Eldridge *Essays in the Sociology of Industrial Relations* (1968), p. 84.

[31] Royal Commission on Trade Unions, etc., Research Paper 4, 'Restrictive Labour Practices', p. 47.

[32] J. Hilton *et al. Are Trade Unions Obstructive?* (1935), p. 333.

on Relations between Employers and Employed recommended in 1917 that in all well-organized industries a system of joint councils be set up, at national, district and workshop levels. Agreements on wages and hours were to be confined to the former, whilst works committees were left to discuss a variety of other matters of local import. In those industries where combinations among workers or employers were inadequate to sustain a voluntary procedure, the committee envisaged that statutory trade boards would be set up with legal powers to enforce minimum wages. Following on these recommendations, between 1917 and 1921 seventy-three National Joint Industrial Councils and thirty-eight new Trade Boards were established.

The optimism which gave birth to this enterprise proved short-lived. Some trade unions, including those in coal mining, engineering and building, rejected 'Whitleyism' either on the grounds that it offered a bogus alternative to more radical solutions including nationalization and workers' control, or because decentralized and disorganized negotiations offered greater rewards. The employers in turn were alarmed at the threatened loss of managerial responsibility; the railway companies accepted national wage bargaining machinery in 1921 only after the Railwaymen's Union had abrogated its claim for 'joint control', and the Engineering Employers' Federation felt impelled to embody the principle of managerial autonomy in the settlement which ended a national lockout in 1922. In other industries, where J.I.C.s had been successfully founded before 1921, they were often destroyed or weakened by the impact of depression and the widespread resort to drastic wage cuts. Their number was down to fifty-one by 1931, and many of these were inactive. The process of decline was accelerated because of the inconsistent nature of government support for national collective bargaining. Whilst the Ministry of Labour had been energetic in promoting Whitley Councils in the immediate post-war years it grew much more passive during the depression; its staff was pruned by the Geddes axe, it ceased to set up Trade Boards, and it failed to give any legal support to voluntary agreements of a kind which might have prevented the disintegration of employers' associations in particular.[33]

At shopfloor level, besides, Whitleyism had never taken root. The recommendation that works committees be established for consultative purposes within the factory was opposed from almost

[33] F. Tillyard and W. A. Robson, 'The Enforcement of the Collective Bargain in Great Britain' (*Economic Journal*, vol. 48, 1938). The trade unions were, admittedly, divided on this question.

every quarter. In those industries, such as engineering, where shop stewards had emerged as a powerful force during the First World War (to be officially recognized by the agreements of 1917 and 1919) local organs of the kind proposed seemed nugatory, shorn of the right to negotiate on wages and conditions and confined to the discussion of non-controversial questions. To the trade union leadership, on the other hand, works committees resembled a possible threat to their own authority, especially since some companies which sponsored them also denied recognition to the unions. So long as their membership continued to fall, moreover, labour officials preferred a strategy of centralized bargaining which would least expose their areas of local weakness. To most employers, finally, shopfloor institutions were an unnecessary encumbrance, or at least became so once the tide of working-class militancy after the Armistice receded under the impact of depression. Managerial interest in the idea of 'worker participation', never very sincere, diminished further in the early 1920s, just as the number of welfare workers employed in British industry rapidly declined. Works committees thus remained, outside the sphere of government departments and the railways, a rare and uncultivated species, even in those industries where N.J.I.C.s existed.

The evident lack of enterprise of management (both employers' associations and individual companies) in the field of industrial relations was also, of course, a reflection of the reduction of strikes. In the immediate post-war period, wage and price instability – and initially a high trade-union membership – had provided a setting for a series of national stoppages, notably in the coal industry. Between 1919 and 1925 an average of 28 million working days a year were lost through strikes and lockouts. After about 1927, however, with the cost of living fluctuating much less sharply and the wage cuts of the earlier depression becoming less frequent, national disputes almost ceased.[34] The average of working days lost in strikes between 1927 and 1939 fell to just over 3 million a year. In that employers tended to regard the avoidance of stoppages as the principal or sole purpose of the industrial relations system, they lost interest in its improvement once this problem receded.

The pattern of inter-war industrial relations thus grew more rigid and unchanging. On the one hand the majority of trade unions,

[34] Macmillan Committee on Finance and Industry, Statement of T.U.C. Evidence, vol. i, pp. 307–12; H. A. Clegg, 'Some Consequences of the General Strike' (*Trans. Manchester Stat. Soc.*, 1954).

especially the large general unions, sought to consolidate the process of national bargaining. Where N.J.I.C.s had survived the post-war slump they were often able to retain their authority, and in such industries this was the period of national negotiations *par excellence*. At the same time, there could be little successful pioneering. Expanding new industries like motor vehicle manufacture remained largely outside the control of the unions, as did service industries like retailing. The government did not help them; having earlier abandoned the extension of Trade Boards and the encouragement of joint councils, it rarely departed from a *laissez-faire* position.[35]

On the employers' side, this was a long-drawn-out period of inertia. Indeed, the passive outlook of industrialists, and especially of the employers' associations, contrasts with the more flexible and self-questioning attitude of the unions, at least as represented by the T.U.C. General Council. After the General Strike the trade union movement professed itself ready to abandon radical anti-capitalist postures (which had in any case often been pietistic) and to invite consultation and co-operation, through specially constructed national machinery, on a variety of topics including rationalization and technological change. Only a minority of employers showed themselves interested, however, and the well-publicized exhibition of friendship and harmony laid on in the 'Mond–Turner' talks had no practical consequence. Most managers in industry continued to complain bitterly about the damaging effects of restrictive practices, but they did little to try and eliminate them beyond dismissing militant shop stewards and unofficial leaders in the period after the General Strike. The coal industry in the 1930s suggested that the cause of labour productivity was not helped by union weakness; but there was little effort to find out (except through such idealistic and atypical methods as co-partnership schemes) what the alternatives were. The research carried out in the United States by Elton Mayo and others on the subject of work group behaviour had little influence in Britain until after the second war. The conduct of wage bargaining followed established principles, with changes linked to cost of living indices or selling price – the London Passenger Transport Board's attempt to bring productivity into this operation was a rare and almost unnoticed experiment.

The decade of the 1940s, however, saw a renewed expansion of national bargaining machinery, both voluntary and statutory, in those fields of industry where it had been lacking hitherto. This

[35] One exception was in the haulage industry, for which see A. Bullock *Life and Times of Ernest Bevin*, vol. i, pp. 618–19.

development was the product of Bevin's policy as wartime Minister of Labour, though it was facilitated by the orders on compulsory arbitration that were in force throughout these ten years. The number of N.J.I.C.s increased to 111 by 1946, and subsequently grew steadily to reach 200 or so by the mid-1960s. Wages Councils replaced the old Trade Boards in 1945, and were extended to cover such major sectors as catering, retailing and road haulage.

The most important changes in industrial relations since 1945, however, have not occurred in this formal context of nationwide collective bargaining, but in the environment of the individual firm or factory. The origins of this transition lie in pre-war developments in industry, the growth then of a number of very large companies, and especially the spread of piecework systems. Incentive wages payments could be successfully maintained and adapted only in a domestic setting. Subsequently the war itself pushed employers in the direction of actual local bargaining on wages, by restoring full employment and union strength, and by demanding that attention be given to the improvement of labour productivity. The factory production committees set up after 1941 were a testimony both to the outdatedness of pre-war methods of industrial discipline and to the constructive possibilities of collaboration with shop stewards in raising efficiency. Simultaneously many firms discovered once again their need for a specialist branch of management to deal with labour and personnel questions.

Nor was there the same reversion to traditional practice after 1945 as had occurred after 1918. The persistence of full employment and high union membership (see Table 23) helped to preserve the importance of shopfloor bargaining. More shop stewards were appointed by the unions, to offset the shortage of permanent officials. The continued popularity of payment by results up to the 1960s, and the rapidity with which technological change affected work processes, gave local representatives plenty of responsibility. National negotiations proved incapable of governing or controlling domestic conditions – as was made apparent, for instance, by the emergence of the phenomenon of 'wage drift', the increase of earnings in excess of what was provided by official agreements.[36] The same tendency towards decentralized wage bargaining was also

[36] Wage drift is not easily defined, since it is not exactly synonymous either with the difference in money terms between basic wages and earnings, or with the difference in their respective rates of increase. For the problem of its measurement see Clegg *System of Industrial Relations*, pp. 293–4. The phenomenon may, of course, have existed in some form in years of full employment prior to 1918.

encouraged by the occasional success of the government – as in 1948–50 – in holding back standard wage increases, and later by the adoption in some industries of long-term national agreements.

These pressures have influenced both the government and the employers in their approach to industrial relations. They have been concerned, from different points of view, by the same problems. Firstly, the rapid increases in earnings, augmented by wage drift, have been regarded as a source of 'cost–push inflation', which in turn has reduced the competitiveness of British industry, especially abroad. Secondly, full employment has highlighted the restraints on production attributable to restrictive labour practices, to which the old remedy of disciplining the unions no longer seems applicable. Thirdly, the devolution of power towards the shop floor has led to a proliferation of unofficial strikes – which since 1945 have vastly outnumbered official stoppages, and to a lesser degree outweighed them as a cause of loss of working time.[37] Although there is not much reason for holding the unofficial strikes of the post-war years to be economically more damaging than the official disputes which predominated in the inter-war period, and which were received with a good deal more fatalism, politicians, managers, the press, and even the Royal Commission have assumed their occurrence to be more unfortunate and their avoidance more imperative.[38]

The government's analysis of this situation impelled it (after several abortive attempts between 1948 and 1964) to launch a prices and incomes policy,[39] and to adopt much of the Report of the Royal Commission on Trade Unions (published in 1968), projecting a general reform of the industrial relations system. The response of the employers to the same problems has been the development of plant- and company-based productivity bargaining, in place of the industry-wide agreements for which employers' associations have been responsible in the past. Public and private policy became linked at this point, as a result of the distinct preference which the National Prices and Incomes Board showed for this form of 'agreement with strings'.[40]

Productivity bargaining has been succinctly defined as a 'first step towards a modern viable system of managerial control over pay and

[37] For statistics, see Royal Commission on Trade Unions, etc., *Report*, pp. 98–100.

[38] For a more sceptical opinion, see H. A. Turner *Is Britain Really Strike-Prone?* and J. E. T. Eldridge *Essays in the Sociology of Industrial Relations.*

[39] For which see Chapter 8.

[40] See N.B.P.I. *Productivity Agreements* (Cmnd. 3311, 1967).

effort'.[41] The first agreement of major importance was negotiated in the Esso refinery at Fawley in 1960. This was followed by other model package deals in the steel, chemicals and oil industries. And their example in turn was followed from the mid-1960s by numerous other firms, so that in July 1969 the Department of Employment and Productivity had registered over 3,000 'productivity agreements' affecting a quarter of the labour force. The majority of these were negotiated locally, although attempts at national bargains have been made in the electricity supply industry and in coal mining.[42] In essence, such agreements have two objects: to provide for the more efficient use of manpower, by reducing overtime, relaxing demarcation rules, introducing work study and so forth; and to eliminate 'wage drift' by the more detailed or exact specification of earnings. Normally productivity agreements offer the wage-earners generous concessions in the form of higher basic rates and reduced hours of work, in return for a written understanding on these subjects.

For a time, productivity bargaining apparently earned the favour of a large number of employers. The real scope of the change in managerial practice was, however, much less impressive. This method of bargaining was in many cases forced upon industry by the exigencies of a restrictive incomes policy, which allowed large wage increases to be conceded only if they were dressed in this kind of garb. As a result, it is clear that many of the agreements so labelled involved no more than the revision of existing pay structures to accord with new methods of production, affecting only marginal changes in restrictive practices. As far as workers are concerned, productivity bargaining is likely to be acceptable in the long run only if it is seen that the financial benefits thus secured are equitably divided.[43] Even then this mode of wage determination, while it may supplement, is unlikely to supersede traditional criteria governing pay awards, like job comparability and the retail price level. In addition, there are some groups of employees who would find difficulty in engaging in this sort of bargaining; and even in cases

[41] A. Flanders, quoted in *Productivity Bargaining* (Royal Commission on Trade Unions, etc., Research Paper 4).

[42] The agreement in the coal industry, however, has proved one of the less successful examples. See R. G. Searle-Barnes *Pay and Productivity Bargaining* (Manchester 1969).

[43] For such considerations, see T. Topham, 'Productivity Bargaining', in *Trade Union Register* (1969); also N. Stettner *Productivity Bargaining and Industrial Change* (1969), p. 110: 'Productivity bargaining is designed as a way of increasing efficiency in the utilisation of manpower, not of improving the distribution of income.'

where workers can justify large rewards by their readiness to accept changes in behaviour and organization, it is likely that sooner or later they will reach a point of diminishing returns. No doubt shopfloor negotiations do hold some of the keys to improved industrial relations and higher labour productivity, but like other such economic remedies they are not self-sufficient – complementing but not replacing labour market policies of training, recruitment and the like.

In some cases at least, however, the short-term success of productivity bargaining has done much to demonstrate the economic costs of bad industrial relations in the past. The main responsibility for curing industrial unrest and restrictive labour practices has always lain with management, for on their own insistence the initiative in promoting efficiency and expansion has been theirs. Neither workers nor unions have these objects as their principal immediate interest, and they cannot be expected to make sacrifices wholly for the sake of others, whether shareholders or the nation. Thus the burden of reconciling workers' interests with those of the firm lies with the most important decision-takers – albeit with increasing help from the government. Yet throughout the period since 1918, as has been seen, the enterprise of management in this regard has been half-hearted; strikes and restrictive practices alike have been blamed on unions and shop stewards, and hence often treated as unavoidable. Thus the indifferent record of Britain in industrial relations no doubt has a part, though clearly varying in extent from one industry and

TABLE 23

Trade Union Membership in the U.K.

Thousands

1914	4,145
1920	8,348
1925	5,506
1930	4,842
1935	4,867
1939	6,298
1945	7,875
1950	9,289
1955	9,741
1960	9,835
1965	10,181
1968	10,049

SOURCE *British Labour Statistics, 1886–1968*, Table 196.

firm to another, in accounting for the sluggish growth of labour productivity since 1918.[44]

ADDITIONAL READING

C. F. CARTER AND B. R. WILLIAMS *Industry and Technical Progress* (1957)

H. A. CLEGG *The System of Industrial Relations in Great Britain* (Oxford 1969)

P. COOK AND R. COHEN *Effects of Mergers* (1958)

A. FLANDERS *Trade Unions* (7th edn, 1968)

P. FORD *The Economics of Collective Bargaining* (2nd edn., Oxford 1964)

J. F. B. GOODMAN AND T. G. WHITTINGHAM *Shop Stewards in British Industry* (1968)

A. F. LUCAS *Industrial Reconstruction and the Control of Competition* (1937)

B. MCCORMICK AND A. SMITH *The Labour Market* (1968)

R. MARRIS *Economic Theory of Managerial Capitalism* (1964)

C. F. PRATTEN 'The Merger Boom in Manufacturing Industry' (*Lloyds Bank Review* 1968)

G. F. RAY 'The Size of Plant: A comparison' (*National Institute Economic Review* 38, 1966)

I. G. SHARP *Industrial Conciliation and Arbitration in Great Britain* (Geneva 1950)

W. G. SHEPHERD 'Changes in British Industrial Concentration, 1951–8' (*Oxford Economic Papers* 18, 1966)

A. SINGH, G. WHITTINGHAM AND H. T. BURLEY *Growth, Profitability and Valuation* (Cambridge 1966)

H. A. TURNER 'Collective Bargaining and the Eclipse of Incomes Policy: Retrospect, Prospect and Possibilities' (*British Journal of Industrial Relations* 8, 1970)

[44] For some discussion of the problem of measuring the effect of restrictive practices and industrial stoppages see L. Ulman, 'Collective Bargaining and Industrial Efficiency' in R. Caves and assoc. *Britain's Economic Prospects* (1968). Unlike the Royal Commission on Trade Unions (*Report*, pp. 111–12) he argues that strikes are likely to hamper bad management rather than good.

CHAPTER 5

Distribution of Income and Growth of Consumer Expenditure

The purpose of this chapter is to analyse the division of the national product whose growth was plotted in Chapter 1 between the factors of production studied in Chapters 2 and 3, and to survey the ways in which the 'personal' part of this income has been spent in the form of domestic consumption. The questions here discussed will to some extent divert us from the theme of economic growth, although of course the changes in the allocation and use of income are themselves aspects of the process of growth, and are influenced by the rate of expansion of the economy. In addition, private consumption is a constituent of total effective demand (statistically the largest constituent) and variations in the level of consumption can therefore certainly have some impact on the behaviour of the economy as a whole. How far personal expenditure has been a strategic influence on economic development since 1918 will be discussed briefly in the conclusion to this chapter.[1]

There are three main approaches to the analysis of national income. The first examines how it is received: the shares going to wages, salaries, profits, self-employed income and rents. The second examines how it is distributed between persons or income units (an inquiry intimately linked with the study of the distribution of wealth). The third approach seeks to show how national income is expended: on personal consumption, on investment, and on public services. We shall look at the results of each of these breakdowns in turn.

Table 24 shows how the national income has been received under different heads since 1900. To observe the most important trends here we may concentrate on three broad income categories: the shares going to labour (comprising both wages and salaries), profits and rents. The problem of explaining the relationship between these elements has exercised economists since Ricardo wrote in 1820, 'Political Economy . . . I think . . . should . . . be called an inquiry

[1] This discussion may be brought together with the remarks on the other elements of 'effective demand', capital formation, foreign trade, and government expenditure, in Chapters 3, 6 and 8 respectively.

into the laws which determine the division of the product of industry amongst the classes who concur in its formation.'[2] The difficulties of discovering them have always been intractable. Even the most up-to-date textbook on labour economics concludes that 'no completely satisfactory theory of income distribution is available'.[3] We shall be satisfied in this discussion, therefore, to eschew general theory, and simply to offer some empirical suggestions as to when and why the most significant changes in income allocation have occurred.

TABLE 24

Distribution of National Income

	Wages	Salaries	Self-employed incomes	Gross trading profits Private	Gross trading profits Public	Rent
1900	41·4	9·1	—	—	—	12·5
1921	43·6	17·9	13·4	5·7	0·5	5·8
1930	39·4	21·1	14·8	11·3	1·2	8·5
1938	40·8	21·9	13·4	14·3	1·4	9·3
1946	48·4	23·4	14·0	18·4	1·3	5·3
1950	44·8	25·5	12·8	19·6	3·0	4·9
1960	42·8	29·2	9·5	17·7	3·4	5·9
1968	40·0	35·4	8·4	15·3	4·3	7·0

[a] Excluding stock appreciation and net property incomes from abroad.

SOURCE Bacon and Bain; C. H. Feinstein in J. Marchal and B. Ducros.

For this purpose it will be convenient for the moment to ignore self-employed incomes, since they represent a mixture of labour income and of profit. This clearly will not affect the upward trend in the share of national income going to earnings from employment, which has risen markedly since the turn of the century from about half to about three-quarters of the total. The periods of most rapid increase in this regard have coincided with the two world wars. In both cases the effect of war and reconstruction was permanently to augment the size of the labour force (especially the salariat) and to bring about a significant growth of real wages. At other times the movement of the labour income component of national income has usually been complicated by the divergent behaviour of wages and salaries.

[2] Quoted in N. Kaldor, 'Alternative Theories of Income Distribution' (in B. J. McCormick and J. E. Owen Smith *The Labour Market* (1968). The whole of Kaldor's article offers a useful introduction to this question.

[3] L. C. Hunter and D. J. Robertson *Economics of Wages and Labour* (1969), p. 387.

Profits did not always fluctuate inversely with labour incomes, and trends in this series are not always easy to explain. The low share of this element in 1921 reflects the abnormal circumstances of the post-war trade depression. Private trading profits increased again relative to other categories especially during the late 1930s and the Second World War, but fell fairly steadily up to the late 1960s. This latter decline is more striking considering that the two decades concerned were a period of price inflation when profits might normally be expected to increase; that the rate of capital formation has risen since the war; and that the element of economic rents contained in profits has presumably moved upwards since 1950 in common with other rents. The latest generation of entrepreneurs have necessarily become accustomed to somewhat lower profit margins than enjoyed in the past – although it is very unlikely that the share of profits has fallen any further since 1968.

The proportion of national income claimed by profits in the post-war generation does, however, seem to have been determined by influences not previously operating. For much of the first half of the twentieth century (and probably during the nineteenth century too) profits grew most rapidly in the national income during periods of rapid inflation and cyclical recovery, when market conditions were relatively 'soft'. This pattern was observable still in 1914–20 and 1933–8. The evident weakening of the connection between prices and profits since the Second World War might be attributable to various factors: to firms working at less than full capacity in conditions of high employment; to higher taxation; to the more effective pressure of trade unions; or to changing managerial attitudes on what constituted an acceptable rate of return. But the subject still awaits a systematic explanation.

After a long period of decline, beginning before 1900, the upturn in the share of rent incomes since 1950 deserves notice. Investment in real property during this period has undoubtedly become more remunerative than investment in most forms of industrial assets. The growing shortage of urban land and the reduction in rent controls during a period of housing shortages after 1958 are among the reasons for this minor economic revolution. In social terms, one of its effects has been the tendency for the private landlord to be superseded by the property company or investment trust; although the predominant (indirect) beneficiaries of increasing rents are still clearly drawn from the upper income groups.

Before considering further this question of income distribution between persons, a final word should be said about the changing composition of labour incomes. The difference between wages, salaries, and the labour element in self-employed incomes is to some extent a social one; the difference between mean *levels* of income in each class has been steadily shrinking for most of the twentieth century. Nevertheless, some differences of statistical behaviour have been evident. In particular, wages have been a much more volatile item than other kinds of remuneration from employment – though remaining a surprisingly stable proportion of national income in the long run. Clearly cyclical fluctuations have had more impact on wage earners than on other social groups; and prior to 1945 wage movements were probably considerably influenced by variations in profits, also a relatively unstable part of national income.

Although money wages can be affected by conditions of labour shortage and trade union strength, it appears from the evidence that the percentage share of wages in the national income can not. Wage-earners seem more certain to gain relatively to other sections of the population (at least if they are in employment) when prices are falling and trade unions weak. Although there were times, in 1945–55 and 1965–8 when the wage share rose along with money wages, these situations seem to be atypical. In the post-war decade the economy was conditioned by government controls; since 1950 the elasticity of wages has probably been due to the rare coincidence of favourable factors: rising productivity, generally full employment, a declining capital/output ratio and advantageous terms of trade.

Salaries have maintained a more uniform share of national income than wages in the short run, but have grown, relatively speaking, much more rapidly during the longer period since 1900. The absence of marked fluctuation has been held to indicate that salaries are regarded by employers as an overhead rather than a prime cost. The lower unemployment rate among salaried workers, apparent in the inter-war years, offers some support for this assumption. Usually, therefore, salaries rose even more than wages as a proportion of national income during periods of deflation, like 1920–4 or (to a lesser extent) 1929–33;[4] but they fell relatively to both wages and profits in times of recovery and price increases, such as 1935–40 and 1949–56. The long-term growth of salaries is principally due to the expansion of the white-collar and professional elements of the occupied population. The size of the salariat rose from 1·67m. in 1911 to 6·93m. in 1961 – accounting for almost 90 per cent of the increase in the labour force during these years. Much of this expan-

[4] The salaries of public servants were cut in 1931 as part of the government's economy drive.

sion has occurred in the manufacturing sector, especially since the Second World War: administrative, technical and clerical staff formed 17·9 per cent of all employees here in 1948 and 27·3 per cent in 1968. In this period, too, the influx into the higher grades has more than kept pace with recruitment to routine non-manual occupations which proliferated so rapidly between the wars.

Distribution of Income and Wealth

Table 25 provides figures relating to the income of taxable units, or families living together, and the wealth of individual adult property owners. The different methods of measurement do not permit exact comparison between the two scales; but the greater and more persistent inequalities of wealth are clear enough, and it has thus rightly been held that to treat income distribution in isolation gives a misleading impression.[5]

TABLE 25

Distribution of Personal Incomes and Wealth

(a) *Income* Shares of given income percentiles after tax

	1949	1963
top 1%	6·4	5·2
top 10%	27·1	25·2
top 40%	64·1	64·7

SOURCE R. J. Nicholson *Lloyds Bank Review* 83, 1967.

(b) *Wealth* Percentile shares of net personal capital

	1911–13	1936	1951–6	1960
top 1%	65·5	59·5	42·0	42·0
top 10%	90·0	88·0	79·0	83·0

SOURCES H. Lydall and Tipping *Bull. Oxf. Univ. Instit. Stats.*, 1961; J. E. Meade *Efficiency, Equality and the Ownership of Property*.

A measure of redistribution of income, and to a lesser extent wealth, has, however, taken place since 1918. This statement holds true whether judged by the share of income and wealth accruing to the richest percentiles of the population (the computation used in the table) or by a calculation of the mean deviation of the curve of actual income distribution from the line of total equality (the so-

[5] Income derived from personal property, moreover, is distributed more unequally than property itself (J. Meade *Efficiency, Equality and the Ownership of Property* (1964), pp. 27–9).

called Gini concentration ratio).[6] The latter device indicates the extent to which incomes have become bunched towards the central rungs of the ladder – a tendency evident in two periods especially, the years during and immediately after the two world wars. In these intervals it appeared both that the rich were losing their advantages in face of rising and steepening taxation; and that differentials of earnings, between skilled and unskilled workers, or wage-earners and salary earners, were diminishing. The reduction of wage differentials has been connected both with the 'dilution' of skilled trades which occurred in wartime, and with the preference which trade unions showed for flat-rate increases covering all grades of workmen. The narrowing of the wage–salary gap (which was not an exactly simultaneous process) owed more to the price movements mentioned earlier. Both these trends, it should be added, were discontinuous: wage differentials widened between 1924 and 1934, and have certainly not lessened during the 1950s and 1960s. The gains made by wages on salaries, as has been seen, occurred only at the very beginning and end of the inter-war period, and the average level of salaries (as well as the share of salaries in the national income) grew faster than wages between 1956 and 1965.

That there has been a proportionate increase in the numbers falling into the middle income groups since 1918 is more or less undisputed. But there is much more controversy about the distribution of income at the extremes: whether the top 10 per cent of the population have suffered so acute a straitening of their circumstances as the statistics suggest; or whether the amount of poverty has fallen since 1918 or since 1945.

The hypothesis that large incomes have been relatively curtailed during the last fifty, and especially during the last thirty, years has been questioned chiefly on the grounds of the inadequacy of the statistics. Three points in particular may be made in this connection. Firstly, the estimates of income distribution provided by the inland revenue authorities are based on the somewhat artificial administrative concept of the 'income unit'. The comparison of income received by different income groups thus relies on the dubious premise that the income units in each group are similarly constituted and evolve in the same way over time. Secondly, the statistics have, especially until recently, seriously underestimated those elements of income such as realized capital gains which derive directly from

[6] For an illustration of the use of this technique, see A. R. Prest and T. Stark, 'Some Aspects of Income Distribution in the U.K. since World War II' (*Manchester School* 35, 1967).

ownership of wealth. Thirdly, the argument for growing equality ignores the problem of tax evasion and of the 'legal arrangement or manipulation of the constituents and sources of spending power' in order to lower tax assessments.[7]

What conclusions can then be drawn, in face of this criticism, about the pattern of income distribution since the First World War? In the inter-war years, between 1921 and 1938, material is sparse. Such evidence as there is points to a fairly slow, though steady, reduction of the share of the richest 10 per cent, which is in keeping with the increases in direct taxation which were imposed during the First World War.[8] Demographic changes in this period were slight and would probably not falsify the trends indicated by assessing income units. On the other hand the changes in the distribution of recorded wealth in this period were almost non-existent. Even allowing for the possibility that methods of tax avoidance may have been less sophisticated and widespread than later, the opportunities for enjoying unassessed income from property remained considerable. Any shift that did occur was thus likely to have been slight.

It is the figures relating to the period between 1938 and 1955, which suggest a substantial relative decline in the highest levels of disposable income, whose accuracy has been most seriously questioned. During these years social and demographic changes took place which might distort the picture presented by inland revenue records. And the increased burden of taxation on incomes and wealth certainly gave incentives to the conspicuously well-off either to emigrate to more indulgent or less necessitous states or to find other means of protecting their finances. It is perhaps difficult to believe that they were completely successful in the latter enterprise, but once again the amount of redistribution was almost certainly well below what the statistical evidence indicates.

Since 1955 or thereabouts material is more plentiful, and if it continues to suffer from some of the deficiencies of earlier records, the greater awareness of these deficiencies has brought an added caution to its interpretation, and even encouraged attempts to build some compensatory mechanisms into its use. In any event, the results of recent inquiries have raised fewer doubts simply because

[7] R. M. Titmuss *Income Distribution and Social Change* (1962), esp. pp. 21–2, 50–2.

[8] Estimates are to be found in: L. R. Connor, 'Aspects of the Distribution of Income in the U.K., 1913 and 1924' (J.R.S.S., 91, 1928); A. L. Bowley *Some Economic Consequences of the Great War* (1930), p. 138; C. Clark *National Income and Outlay* (1938), pp. 105–10; T. Barna *Redistribution of Incomes through Public Finance in 1937* (Oxford 1945).

they have shown, since the end of the 1950s, little or no further levelling of incomes. This may be due in part to the effects of earlier redistribution on the taxable capacity of the rich, but there is little doubt that the increase of income from property (such as rent) and the deliberate reduction of the level of taxation in the highest incomes (partly to rectify what was supposed to be excessive egalitarianism) played an important role.

Another perspective on income distribution is afforded by the study of poverty. Here a problem of definition arises: 'poverty' is a term as amorphous as 'wealth', but a social problem more in need of active redress. Throughout the inter-war years, the poor were designated as those families whose income left them on or below a fixed line of subsistence. But the assessment of adequate subsistence itself raised difficulties. In addition, the local character of most social surveys of poverty between 1918 and 1939 gave rise to conclusions of considerable, and not altogether credible, disparity. Bowley and Hogg, investigating five medium-sized towns in 1923, found 8 per cent of working-class families to be on or below their poverty line.[9] Other surveys, on a similar basis, put forward figures of 17·3 per cent for Merseyside in 1929, 31 per cent for York in 1936, and 10·7 per cent for Bristol in 1937. No national inquiry was conducted before the wa.; the Ministry of Labour organized a family expenditure survey in 1937/8, but deliberately excluded the families of the long-unemployed, obviously liable to poverty, from its coverage.

Since the Second World War the view of what constituted poverty has altered radically. This was particularly the case from the mid-1950s onwards, when the shortcomings of welfare legislation based upon the old idea of a subsistence minimum and the rapid increase in average incomes enjoyed by the bulk of the working class made the earlier definitions seem especially inadequate. One new approach has been to accept the scales used by the National Assistance Board as an index, a flexible gauge in that the scales rose roughly in proportion to average industrial earnings during the 1950s, and to estimate the numbers whose income or expenditure was less than 40 per cent above this standard. The criterion of subsistence has been thereby replaced by what might be regarded as a measure of poverty defined by current cultural or social norms. 7·8 per cent of the population fell below this standard in 1953/4 (estimated in terms of their average weekly expenditure) and 14·2 per cent in 1960 (estimated on the basis of average income).[10] A second study using the same

[9] A. L. Bowley and M. H. Hogg *Has Poverty Diminished?* (1925).
[10] P. Townsend and B. Abel-Smith *The Meaning of Poverty* (1965).

method of definition but employing income tax data rather than survey material, showed a decline in the proportion of sub-marginal incomes between 1954 and 1959, but a slight increase by 1963, the percentages being 21·0, 18·1, and 20·7 respectively.[11]

The survival of poverty amid affluence is only in part a problem of administering welfare benefits. It is true that a large proportion of those in poverty could probably have been rescued by higher old-age pensions, unemployment benefits or family allowances. But the predicament of some at least of those who suffer from 'relative deprivation' derives from an apparent failure of their earnings from employment to keep pace with those of fellow-workers or with the cost of living. The tendency for material progress to overlook a certain minority of society, which has been noted also in the United States for example,[12] appears thus far to be insoluble. The neglect of trade unions has been offset neither by the partial success of statutory wages councils nor the recent abortive attempt at an incomes policy.

The Growth of Personal Consumption

Economists have given only a limited amount of attention to the problem of the relationship between private consumption, income distribution and economic growth. It is true that studies of the long-term changes in the pattern of consumption have been carried out, and used for the purpose of predicting future trends. The emphasis of such inquiries, however, has been laid on the stability of consumption habits from one generation to the next, and on the cumulative nature of such variations as are found. Yet it has been obvious both before the Second World War and since that short-term fluctuations in consumer demand and in the marginal propensity to consume can be of a fairly high order. What is more, on particular occasions these fluctuations have been given as the explanation of broader economic trends: of the recovery from the slump during the 1930s, and of the failure of the economy to grow more rapidly during the 1960s.

The rules which govern the normal behaviour of consumers are, so far as they are understood, comparatively easily rehearsed. Marginal propensity to consume varies inversely with the size of income. Hence the redistribution of income towards the lower income groups tends, other things being equal, to raise the level of consumption. Not only will wage-earners spend more of their

[11] I. Gough and T. Stark, 'Low Incomes in the U.K., 1954, 1959 and 1963' (MS 36, 1968).

[12] M. Harrington *The Other America* (2nd edn, 1969).

receipts, but those in higher income brackets will not necessarily spend less, even if they suffer a loss in real income, unless this is accompanied by a simultaneous reduction of wealth. If redistribution takes place in favour of the rich, on the other hand, this leads to increased saving if the increment is in the form of income, but to increased spending if it is in the form of wealth.

Long-term changes in the pattern of consumption during the twentieth century, however, can probably be explained without reference to redistribution, but simply by the cumulative growth of real income *per capita*, and by certain accompanying economic and social changes. Personal expenditure at constant prices grew by 72 per cent between 1900 and 1960, but only 30 per cent *per capita.* Most of this increase occurred in the 1930s and the 1950s. The acceleration of consumption has been maintained between 1960 and 1968, when the real growth of private expenditure ran at the rate of nearly 2·4 per cent a year.

A significant part of the change in consumer habits during this period has consisted of shifts in the demand for goods within individual commodity groups. Thus the proportion of disposable income spent on food was almost the same in 1955 as it had been in 1900, although clearly less of this went on necessities and more on luxury or labour-saving items. The importance of domestic service has declined rapidly, whereas the demand for household durables has risen sharply, first in the inter-war years and again since 1950.[13] The consumption of alcohol and tobacco together has shown a steady decline in the average budget since 1900, though this was very sharply reversed during the brief period of the Second World War; but this change conceals a fairly continuous reduction in expenditure on drink partly offset by a fairly steady increase, until recently, of percentage expenditure on tobacco. Finally, whereas the initial growth of demand for entertainment during and after the First World War was largely accounted for by cinema attendances, this expenditure has fallen by nearly nine-tenths between 1953 and 1968, and the stability of the item of entertainment in the average budget has been maintained by increases elsewhere, especially in betting.

Two items of consumption may be singled out, however, as reflecting and assisting the industrial developments of the twentieth century. The consumption of electricity has risen rapidly throughout

[13] For domestic servants, see Chapter 3, p. 36. The actual number of domestic servants did not fall between the wars, although many more were employed on a part-time basis. The number employed fell by two-thirds between 1938 and 1955, however.

TABLE 26

Consumer Expenditure, 1900–68

Percentage of total family expenditure on various items

	1900	1920	1938	1950	1968
Food	32·7	33·9	29·2	31·1	26·4
Transport and communications	5·3	5·2	7·7	6·8	13·1
Durable household goods	3·5*	5·3*	6·2*	5·9*	6·7
Drink and tobacco	13·2	11·3	10·5	16·8	9·3
Entertainment	2·5	2·8	3·4	3·9	3·6

* Figures for years 1901–4, 1920–4, 1935–8, 1946–50 respectively.

SOURCES Rowe, 'Private Consumption', in Beckerman *et al. British Economy in 1975*; Stone *et al. Measurement of Consumers' Expenditure and Behaviour in the U.K.*; and *Family Expenditure Survey, 1968.*

this period, initially as a source of fuel and light, since the 1930s as a form of power for radios, vacuum cleaners, televisions and refrigerators. The one million units consuming electricity in 1920 had become ten million by 1939 and seventeen million by 1965 (of which fifteen million were private households). The amount spent on electricity rose more than fourfold between 1945 and 1965, although the rate of growth in real value showed the first signs of decline from about 1963.[14] Expenditure on motor cars and motor cycles also started to go up from the 1920s, although it was only 3·3 per cent of total personal consumption in 1938. The figure remained so modest perhaps because the market created by rapidly reducing prices of vehicles was curtailed by the more inelastic costs of running and repairs. Between 1945 and 1955, however, expenditure on this item increased more than twelve times, and it was the preponderant item of the family 'travel' budget of 1968.

Such long-term shifts in consumption have obviously promoted the growth of output in particular sectors of the economy. But have they helped growth in general? Has the pressure of consumer demand, that is to say, done more to stimulate productivity and efficiency than the fairly slow rate of growth of aggregate personal expenditure would appear to suggest?

It might be possible, over a long period, to demonstrate a correlation between changes in the rates of consumer demand as between different industries and changes in their rates of growth. Although

[14] The increase in expenditure (at constant 1963 prices) was £184m. in 1958–62, and £103m. in 1963–8 (National Income and Expenditure 1969).

this exercise has never been done, it is accepted on a common-sense level that the pressure of demand is connected with productivity, and that consumers have been inclined to purchase the goods of industries or services with superior actual and potential growth records.[15] One group of industries fulfilling this criterion very well were the so-called 'new industries' of the 1930s, and the stimulus given to their growth by the shift of consumer habits during that decade has been given as perhaps the main reason for the buoyancy of the British economy (compared with the economies of other Western nations) during and after the inter-war depression.

The crux of this argument is that an increase in the marginal propensity to consume occurred as a result of the fall in prices and the redistribution of income between 1929 and 1933. This promoted investment and growth in a variety of consumer industries manufacturing electrical and other household goods, motor cars and the like, on a sufficient scale to outweigh the disinvestment and contraction which took place in the staple industries. A structural change in the balance of the economy was brought about, in addition to the normal 'cyclical' recovery of the mid-1930s.[16]

A thesis of this kind is attractive as explaining the somewhat anomalous behaviour of the British economy during and after the inter-war depression. It fails, however, to dispose of the concomitant question, why real incomes in Britain were maintained at a higher level than elsewhere in the industrialized world. In addition, as regards its treatment of consumption, two points may be made. Firstly, it should be noticed that whereas the marginal propensity to consume did rise during the Great Depression, the actual rate of growth of consumer expenditure was lower than immediately before or afterwards. The emphasis placed upon demand as a determinant of high investment thus depends on the argument that consumption became heavily concentrated on a number of strategic industries. There is partial, but hardly overwhelming, evidence for making this assumption. Secondly, the connection between shifts in consumption and the redistribution of income in these years is rather obscure. Although there is good reason to suppose that wage-earners came to form a more important element of a 'mass market' at this time, it

[15] This generalization applies to manufacturing rather than to other sectors of the economy: there was no improvement in the productivity of public utilities, little in that of services, and a deterioration in that of the construction industry, during the inter-war period (J. A. Dowie, 'Growth in the Interwar Period' (*Econ. Hist. Rev.*, 21, 1968).

[16] H. W. Richardson *Economic Recovery in Britain, 1932–9* (1967), pp. 97–123; see also his 'New Industries between the Wars' (*Oxford Econ. Pap.* 13, 1961).

is not clear how far they created the demand for the goods of the new industries upon which economic recovery and growth was based. If the consumption of private houses and cars was primarily attributable to the middle classes, then the effects accounted to the rise in real wages are correspondingly less significant.

The role of consumer demand in the economy during the 1950s and 1960s has been differently interpreted. The world market and international trade have expanded in the recent period, as they did not in the 1930s. It has thus been widely assumed, not least by successive governments, that a high level of domestic consumption is inimical to exports, and thus to the balance of payments. Another distinction, not altogether consistent with the first, has been made between these two periods – that whereas before the Second World War private spending followed a fairly smooth and predictable path, it has since risen much more erratically. During this period the Chancellor of the Exchequer has sought to control the level of demand by such monetary devices as hire purchase restrictions and credit squeezes, effective in the short term but fostering an atmosphere of uncertainty which has hindered growth. Policy decisions have not been helped, of course, by the doubt which persists over the relationship between production for exports and production for the home market. But most economists would probably agree that the consequences of unstable movements in private expenditure have been a liability in both spheres; that, as Professor Dow suggests: 'Since the *alterations* of policy were probably to some extent disrupting, the preservation of a steady but lower pressure of demand might even have resulted in faster growth.'[17]

It is, perhaps, open to question whether faster growth will in fact restore stability to our economic life. Ironically, the macroeconomic theory which economists have applied and elaborated over the last generation was one which sought to locate and explain a deficiency of demand and the consequent waste of productive resources. As a result, it sometimes appears doubtful whether we have fully come to terms with the laws which govern an affluent consumer society. The values and expectations of British society have changed so vastly since the 1930s, that its further economic development must inevitably be difficult to forecast. The complex of problems with which we are presently faced, including the evident failure of a national incomes policy, the rapidity of wage and price inflation, the persistence of a relatively high level of unemployment,

[17] J. C. R. Dow *The Management of the British Economy, 1945–60* (Cambridge, N.I.E.S.R. 1965), p. 361.

and the constant dilemma of government in seeking to promote expansion through imposing restraint, may indeed be temporary, as is still hoped. But these conditions also may prove, at least in part, to be the intrinsic features of modern economic life, no less than poverty, *laissez-faire* and the trade cycle were the hallmarks of previous eras.

ADDITIONAL READING

J. EDMONDS AND G. RADICE *Low Pay* (Fabian Research Series 270)

J. MARCHAL AND B. DUCROS *The Distribution of National Income* (1963)

R. J. NICHOLSON 'The Distribution of Personal Income' (*Lloyds Bank Review*, 83, 1967)

E. H. PHELPS BROWN AND M. H. BROWNE *A Century of Pay* (1968)

E. H. PHELPS BROWN AND P. E. HART 'The Share of Wages in the National Income' (*Economic Journal*, vol. 62, 1952)

G. ROUTH *Occupation and Pay in Great Britain, 1906–60* (1965)

D. A. ROWE 'Private Consumption' (in W. Beckerman *The British Economy in 1975*)

R. STONE *et al. The Measurement of Consumer Expenditure and Behaviour in the United Kingdom, 1920–38* (2 vols, Cambridge 1954 and 1966)

R. STONE 'Private Saving in Britain, Past, Present and Future' (*Manchester School* 32, 1964)

P. TOWNSEND 'The Meaning of Poverty' (*British Journal of Sociology* 13, 1962)

CHAPTER 6

International Trade and Growth

International trade has traditionally been of great strategic importance in the growth and development of the modern British economy. The initial impetus to the rapid and sustained development which occurred and transformed Britain in the second half of the eighteenth century was given by the thrust of international trade, which Britain, for a variety of reasons, was advantageously situated to exploit. This is not to say that domestic factors were unimportant in providing a base for this expansion, simply that the dynamic element appears to have been the foreign sector. Indeed, using Rostovian terminology, it has been claimed that if there existed a 'leading sector' at all in the economy at that time, that sector must have been international trade.

Similarly the substantial reduction in the growth rate which occurred in Britain at the end of the nineteenth century has also been attributed in large measure to the failure of the foreign trade sector to maintain its previous rate of expansion in the face of new and changing conditions of world trade. At all events there was, as Deane and Cole suggest, 'evidently a close relationship between the changing rate of British economic growth and the volume of her international trade'.[1]

The classical theory of comparative cost holds that all states engaged in international trade may benefit through trade and specialization, enabling them to move to higher levels of real income. The requirement is that the participating countries must specialize in the production and export of those commodities in whose production they have the greatest comparative advantage. The key is obviously international specialization. Throughout the nineteenth and early twentieth centuries this was believed to be particularly useful in explaining broad categories of trade such as that between manufacturing and primary-producing countries.

The basic pattern was in outline quite simple. Certain countries,

[1] P. Deane and W. A. Cole *British Economic Growth 1688–1959* (Cambridge 1962), p. 312.

for example Britain, for various reasons had a comparative advantage in the production of manufactured goods. The existence of demand, potential or actual, for these goods induced these countries to transfer resources away from agriculture to the production of manufactured goods. The excess over what was wanted for domestic consumption was exported. A parallel movement of specialization was, however, occurring contemporaneously in the primary producing countries of the world. These, concentrating on the production of foodstuffs or raw materials as the case may be, absorbed the excess of the manufactured products, in return supplying the manufacturing countries with food and raw materials, which after specialization they were unable to produce for themselves.

Thus by the nineteenth century international trade had become an 'engine for growth'[2] which had a cumulative dynamic effect on the economies concerned, inducing a continuous process of specialization and expansion.

This in turn led to a concomitant increase in investment, both domestic and foreign. Investment, it is claimed, is limited by the extent of the market, so that anything which increases the size of the market will, *ipso facto*, induce investment which is almost certainly a prerequisite for growth. Because of this latter effect, the influence of trade on development was certainly far more powerful than the static analysis of comparative cost would initially indicate.

Due in large measure to the continuous process of international specialization and hence of growth of real income, world trade grew very rapidly in the second half of the nineteenth century, at an annual average rate of 3·4 per cent per annum. Britain as the then most industrialized country of the world undoubtedly benefited from this high rate of expansion. At their peak (as a measured percentage of G.N.P.) in the 1870s and 1880s exports averaged roughly 23 per cent and imports 36 per cent of G.N.P. Imports of food and raw materials accounted for 75 per cent of total imports, and exports of manufactured goods accounted for 90 per cent of total exports. But even within the category of manufactured goods Britain had specialized even further so that by 1913 exports of textile manufactures including clothing, iron and steel manufactures including engineering products and coal, accounted for 53 per cent of total exports. Of the total exports 71 per cent were destined for the primary producing countries of the world.

However great the potential benefit from international trade, the country concerned must be able to adapt its economy to the changing

[2] D. H. Robertson *Essays in Monetary Theory* (1940), p. 214.

economic conditions. As the first country to industrialize, Britain, as we have seen, had concentrated heavily on the production of fairly crude and easily manufactured commodities. Other countries following in Britain's path devoted their first efforts to the same products and were thus in direct competition with Britain. Cheap factor supplies (apart from capital) allowed them to produce such goods more cheaply. In retrospect it is clear that Britain should have transferred resources to the production of more capital intensive commodities or those incorporating a high degree of productive skill or expertise, advantages which her initial lead had given her.[3] This she failed to do.

Thus from the end of the nineteenth century exports lost that buoyancy which had characterized them throughout the earlier part of the century, and the whole economy began to grow more slowly. By the 1860s exports were increasing at an annual average rate of 8 per cent; by the beginning of the twentieth century this had fallen to an average annual rate of 1 per cent per annum.

Britain's position in the world economy at the outbreak of World War I was thus a precarious one, exposed to unsolved difficulties of long standing. During and after the war these long-term problems intensified, and further, short-term factors came to exercise an adverse influence on British trade. The industrial development of other national economies continued and often accelerated at the expense of the British economy.

TABLE 27

United Kingdom's Share of World Trade[a]

	1913	1929	1937
World trade quantum	100	133	128
U.K. exports quantum	100	82	72
U.K. share of world trade	14	11	10

[a] A. Lewis *Economic Survey 1919–1939* (1949), p. 79.

India and Japan for instance expanded their textile industries behind tariff barriers and with the help of abundant supplies of cheap labour were able to take over large sections of Britain's traditional markets. The textile industry was more vulnerable in the export field, allegedly, because its characteristics included 'an excessive number of small weak firms . . . and almost fanatical

[3] In a sense, the export of capital may be partly this – exporting financial skills, e.g. the City.

individualism'.[4] The following tables give an indication of the loss of overseas markets.

TABLE 28

Production and Export of Cotton Goods[a]

	Yarn (mill. lb)		Piece goods	
	Prod.	Expt.	Prod.	Expt.
1912	1982	244	8,050	6,913
1930	1047	137	3,500	2,472
1938	1070	123	3,126	1,494

Cotton Piece Goods (Mill. Linear Yards)

	Av. 1909–13	1938	Change
Indian home production	1,141	4,250	+3,109
Total imports into India	2,741	724	−2,017
Of which from U.K.	2,669	158	−2,411
Of which from Japan	4	441	+ 437

[a] S. Pollard *The Development of the British Economy 1914–67* (1962), p. 121.

It is readily apparent that the amount by which Indian home production and Japanese exports to India were increased was almost equivalent to and probably accounted for the fall in the figures of British exports. The other British export industries suffered a similar fate. Exports of coal fell drastically from a figure of 100 million tons in 1913 to 50 million tons in 1927–30. The development of new coalfields, e.g. in East and Central Europe, with wider and easily worked seams, was simply one cause of the growing comparative disadvantage of many of Britain's staple industries and was of course a normal feature of economic development. However, relatively little was done in the form of technical innovation to overcome or at least reduce these natural handicaps. The rate of growth of productivity in the British coal industry lagged behind those of many other countries. Between 1913 and 1936 output per man in Britain increased by 10 per cent, in Holland by 117 per cent and in the Ruhr by 81 per cent.

There were, however, other factors in its decline which were outside the industry's control, the most crucial being the secular reduction in the rate of growth of demand for coal products. Whereas in the period before 1913 world demand for coal increased at an annual average rate of 4 per cent per annum, between 1913 and 1937 the rate had fallen to 0·3 per cent per annum.

[4] A. E. Kahn *Great Britain in the World Economy* (1969) p. 98.

The story of coal and cotton was repeated with more or less emphasis in other sectors of the economy. Between 1921 and 1937 exports of iron and steel fell by 22 per cent, machinery by 39 per cent, shipbuilding by 86 per cent and wool by 41 per cent in value terms. In sum exports had manifestly ceased to be an 'engine for growth' as far as Britain was concerned.

The problems of the exporting industries were further increased because for almost the whole of the inter-war period the primary producing countries experienced a secular decline in the terms of trade of their exports *vis-à-vis* their imports. Thus the relative value of one unit of export became less, and this inevitably led to a reduction in the growth of real income of such countries. British exports were disproportionately concentrated towards primary producing countries, and the reduction in the growth of real income hit British exporters all the harder.

Of the short-term factors affecting Britain's trade performance, possibly the most important was the instability of international exchange rates.

By the turn of the century the world monetary system, the Gold Standard, had acquired a solidity and sophistication which both fostered confidence and allowed countries to specialize more than otherwise would have been the case. After the vicissitudes of the war Britain decided to go off the Gold Standard in 1919 as the only alternative to drastic deflation. It was, however, generally accepted that this would be only temporary, and following a favourable movement on the exchanges Britain did eventually return to the Gold Standard in 1925 at the pre-war rate of $4.86 to the £1. Keynes maintained at the time[5] that this resulted in an overvaluation of the pound by as much as 10 per cent, a view which has been generally accepted to this day (though without much evidence). Some degree of overvaluation there was, however, and this did create further barriers to the ailing exports. It had its most important effect, however, not on the old-established export industries, but on the new potential exports. These failed to respond to the general upsurge of world prosperity in the late 1920s, partly no doubt because of the added burden of uncompetitiveness imposed upon them by the decision to return to Gold. The new industries did not grow rapidly enough in absolute terms to absorb the resources made redundant by declining industries. The result inevitably was unemployment.

Whilst exports were undergoing a long period of decline in the

[5] J. M. Keynes, 'The Economic Consequences of Mr Churchill' in *Essays in Persuasion* (1931). See also Chapter 8.

inter-war years, imports were maintained at their previous high levels which, unless corrective action were taken, would lead to excessive trade deficits. The balance of payments was further worsened by monetary factors so that external equilibrium could only be created by holding down the level of domestic activity. Because of the sluggish condition of the economy the marginal efficiency of capital must have been reduced and the incentive to instal new machinery correspondingly weakened. The adoption of deflationary policies by governments did not solve any of the long-term problems. Production was not diverted to the export sector, which remained depressed, and no marked attempt was made to render British industry more efficient by stimulating investment for long-term growth.

Thus the foreign trade sector was one of unrelieved gloom. Exports declined in importance in the national economy. Whereas even as late as 1920 exports still accounted for as much as 23 per cent of National Income, by 1930 this had fallen to 18 per cent, and to 10 per cent by 1939.

Even so it was obviously still a comparatively strategic sector, so that the breakdown of the world economy after 1930 which had a profoundly depressing effect on exports had negative multiplier reactions right through the economy. One of the more noticeable effects of the world depression of the 1930s was that trade declined far more than did world production.

TABLE 29

World Production and Trade 1929–37[a]

	1929	1932	1937
Foodstuffs			
World trade	100	89	94
World production	100	100	108
Raw materials			
World trade	100	82	108
World production	100	74	116
Manufactures			
World trade	100	57	87
World production	100	70	120

[a] Lewis, op. cit., p. 58.

As can be seen, manufactures, Britain's predominant exports, were affected much more than either of the other two categories of foreign trade. Total exports fell in value from £729m. in 1929 (which was a comparatively low figure anyway) to £365m. in 1932; in quantity terms they fell by 34 per cent. Though there was some recovery from the nadir of 1932, not till after World War II was the 1929 level of exports reached again.

The depression affected imports in a different way. In value terms they declined by much the same proportion (about 50 per cent) to 1937. In quantity terms they were maintained at around the 1929 level, and remained there throughout the recovery. The recorded decline in value must therefore have been due to the fall in import prices. Prices of food and raw materials fell, so that the terms of trade moved rapidly in Britain's favour in the early thirties. Though there was some adverse movement subsequently, the terms of trade continued to favour Britain compared with the 1929 ratio, and were to prove an important factor in the recovery of the economy in this period.

TABLE 30

Terms of Trade Figures for Britain 1913 = 100[a]

1913	= 100
1919	= 142
1920	= 154
1921	= 174
1922	= 160
1923	= 151
1924	= 151
1925	= 145
1926	= 149
1927	= 147
1928	= 144
1929	= 145
1930	= 156
1931	= 174
1932	= 172
1933	= 181
1934	= 171
1935	= 171
1936	= 168
1937	= 159
1938	= 174

[a] Monthly Digest of Statistics, Central Statistical Office.

This was the continuation of long-term forces at work in the international economy. Due to increased productivity, and an increase in the actual number of countries producing food and raw materials, there was a serious situation of overproduction of many products. On the other hand demand failed to grow correspondingly;

in Britain for instance, a major buyer, due to the sluggish performance of the economy. The combined effect was to reduce the price of food and raw materials on world markets. Though prices of manufactured goods also fell, they did so to a far lesser extent and as the table indicates the terms of trade moved considerably in favour of manufacturing countries. Britain, being such a major importer of primary products, benefited more than most from this movement. Between 1929 and 1933 the same volume of exports enabled Britain to obtain 20 per cent more imports.

So far we have examined the empirical evidence on British overseas trade largely by reference to the quantities and value of particular exports and imports. Another and equally revealing approach, however, involves an analysis of changes in the level and distribution of world income. From this vantage it is possible to see the trend of British exports as the outcome of movements of aggregate world income, and of the income elasticity of demand for British products. In similar fashion the trend of British imports is dependent on the aggregate real income of the country and the elasticity of demand for foreign goods.

In the case of Britain this form of analysis can serve to illuminate both the contrasting behaviour of British exports and imports in the inter-war years and the significance as a climacteric of the slump of 1929–33. On the one hand it will be observed from Table 5 that British exports in the 1930s fell in volume more quickly than world trade while the level of imports remained almost static. To a less pronounced extent this pattern was already visible in the 1920s.

TABLE 31

Quantum of British Trade 1929–38[a]

	Exports (1929 = 100)		Imports (1929 = 100)
	Vol. of exports	Vol. of world trade	Vol. of imports
1929	100	100	100
1930	82	93	97
1931	62	85	100
1932	62	74	87
1933	63	75	88
1934	67	78	93
1935	72	81	93
1936	74	85	100
1937	80	96	106
1938	71	88	101

[a] H. W. Richardson *Economic Recovery in Britain 1932–1939* (1967), p. 49.

What it reflects probably is that Britain's heavy reliance on manufactures as exportable commodities made her more susceptible to any fall in world income since the income elasticity of demand for manufacturers was high. Even when world income was growing during the later 1920s, Britain suffered the ill-effects of dependence on primary producing markets whose prosperity was relatively low. On the other hand British imports consisted largely of food and raw materials, and were liable to adjust themselves to fluctuations in income. Britain had little choice but to maintain her level of purchases from abroad or suffer a fall in the standard of living. Though there were compensations against the worst consequences of this dependence, for instance, as has been seen, the advantageous terms of trade enjoyed in the period, the balance of trade position throughout the period continued in substantial deficit.

TABLE 32

Britain's Balance of Trade 1929–38[a]

	£
1929	−259
1930	−282
1931	−323
1932	−217
1933	−196
1934	−221
1935	−185
1936	−260
1937	−339
1938	−284

[a] Richardson, op. cit., p. 48.

At the same time the relationship between Britain and the world economy changed significantly between the 1920s and the 1930s. In the earlier decade Britain had appeared at a disadvantage, failing to enjoy her relative share of the growth of world income. Thereafter, however, world income both fell more quickly than Britain's during the depression and recovered more slowly during the middle and late 1930s. Seen purely from an international perspective the state of the British economy was less disquieting in the second half of the period than in the first.

This view of Britain's foreign trade history between the wars can also be logically connected with her international commercial policy. Although free trade dogma had been attacked as early as the 1880s and various minor breaches forced between 1916 and 1929 (see for example Chapter 8), the decisive victory of protection came only in 1932. Its triumph at that point can be understood both as a response to a worsening balance of payments situation originating in the divergent trends of imports and exports; and also as an attempt to insulate this country from a slump that was more critical and disastrous abroad than at home. In short Britain abandoned a policy of maximizing world income in favour of one of redistributing that income to her own advantage. Even if this invited tariff competition with other countries it was theoretically possible to increase real income.

On the other hand the comprehensive tariff of 1932 could scarcely be said to be a growth policy. For this we have to look back to the more limited experiments in protection begun in the 1920s. Then, for a variety of reasons (some non-economic), it was believed desirable to protect some new industries from their more competitive longer-established foreign rivals. They were unlikely to survive on their own, but their survival was regarded as important by the authorities. The official reasons given were what in effect amounted to infant industry arguments. This was so in the case of glass, synthetic dyestuffs, etc. These protected industries did in fact turn out to be high growth industries, which may well have justified their protection and the misallocation of resources this implies.[6] The costs may in fact have been less than expected due to the existence of unemployed factors of production in the economy. Although it is impossible to be absolutely precise, it does seem the tariffs of the 1920s, minor excursions into protection that they were, were beneficial to growth.

The general tariff of 1932, which was both comprehensive and high, in contrast, may have been negative in its impact, for there is no doubt that tariffs reduced the level of world trade. This is undoubtedly a case where the 'prisoners' dilemma' concept may be useful: whereas each country may have been aware that tariffs if generally adopted might injure all concerned, not one could or would take unilateral action in reducing tariff barriers for fear that other

[6] Although it is difficult to generalize from the experience of others, the history of Germany and U.S.A. prior to World War I and of Japan after World War II justifies a belief in the growth-promoting possibilities of tariff protection.

It may be pointed out that there is a much stronger case for the tariffs in 1920 than that proposed by Chamberlain in the 1890s. He probably would have supported the then declining industries, coal, textiles, etc., which would have slowed down the necessary movement of factors to the new industries which should have occurred. At least in the 1920s the 'correct' industries were protected, though it is difficult to measure its impact.

countries would not respond. On the other hand tariffs could be used as powerful bargaining weapons in trade negotiations with other countries. In particular Britain used this to quite considerable effect in the bilateral trade agreements she negotiated in the 1930s. Compared with most other countries Britain placed few prohibitive restrictions on imports, and the threat of the loss of the British market was often a potent one. Thus Britain was able to obtain favourable terms from trade treaties with Scandinavia, Eastern Europe and South American countries. Since she tended to run a trade deficit with these countries the threat to reduce imports to the value of exports to each country normally gained some concessions for Britain.

The impact of the general tariff was in some cases reduced by the granting of tariff preferences. These were given mainly to Commonwealth countries or countries which had especially close trading connections with Britain. In 1932 the Commonwealth preference system was formalized following the Ottawa agreement, and as the system of Imperial Preference became institutionalized the non-Commonwealth members tended to drop out of the system. On the whole Britain did maintain, and in some instances increase, her trade with the members of this system. However, it is probable that this increase was at the expense of trade with other countries – non-members, as they formed preferential trading agreements amongst themselves. The net effect is likely to have been very small.

It remains now to attempt some broad assessment of the effects which the declining value of British exports had on the growth of the economy. Throughout the 1920s British exports had not only fallen as a percentage of world trade, they had also become less important in the creation of the domestic national income.

TABLE 33

Exports as % of G.N.P.[a]

	Exports (1) £m.	G.N.P. (2) £m.	(1) as % of (2)
1913	525	2765	23%
1929	729	4178	17%
1938	470	4671	10%

[a] H. W. Arndt *The Economic Lessons of the 1930s: A Report* (1944), chapter 4.

The economy was becoming more orientated towards domestic needs, a trend which the depression and associated features obviously enhanced. By the 1930s, therefore, events abroad were less important than in the past in determining the level of economic activity and rate of growth. On the other hand while it is once again impossible to draw any positive conclusion, it seems likely that the terms of trade movement throughout the 1930s were of net benefit to Britain in increasing real income at home. (The effect of the terms of trade in stimulating the growth of new industries is dealt with in Chapter 3.)

What had happened by the late 1930s therefore was a complete reversal of the traditional sequence of economic growth in Britain. International trade had now wholly ceased to be a stimulus to economic expansion, instead growth was increasingly dependent on the buoyancy of the domestic market. And that market was now deliberately protected and fostered by restrictions on the natural flow of trade.

The Second World War might have been expected, on the face of it, to accentuate this tendency. The trading countries of the world were disrupted more completely even than in 1914–18. Following a long period of economic nationalism and tariff warfare, this disturbance foreshadowed apparent disaster. In the event, however, since the late 1940s international trade has proved to be buoyant and expansionary.

Between 1952 and 1964 world trade increased at an annual average rate of 9 to 10 per cent per annum compared with an annual rate of increase of about 2½ per cent per annum previously and once again becomes an 'engine for growth'.

Why should there have been this great expansion in world trade when conditions appeared, on the face of it, to be so unfavourable? It is obviously superficial to say, as some have, that trade increased because of high growth in the industrialized countries, for high growth was in part a direct result of the growth of trade. The interrelationship is more complex.

The classical theory of international trade, that of comparative advantage, was, whether explicitly stated or implicitly assumed, designed to explain trade between two broad groups of countries, manufacturing and primary producing countries. The primary producing countries exported food and raw materials to the manufacturing countries, which being specialized could not produce enough of these commodities to meet their own needs. In exchange they bought manufactured products; and both groups of countries benefited from trade and international specialization. This rather simple analysis, however, does not adequately explain the pattern of trade in a world increasingly dominated by the developed industrialized countries. Due to their great strategic importance in the trading system, these nations determine to a large extent both the pattern and level of world trade. It appears that increasingly since 1945 the dynamic element in this system is the trade which the industrial nations carry on with one another. Although there must obviously be trade between the manufacturing and primary producing countries, this is not so vital as was once thought to be the case. S. Linder,[7] for instance, suggests that the most important determinant of trade is demand, in particular what he calls representative demand. There must be a sufficiently extensive domestic demand for a commodity before manufacturers will risk producing that commodity on a significant scale. Manufacturers produce initially for the home market. Once they establish themselves, and begin to enjoy the fruits of specialization and large-scale production, they will look for foreign markets, but this is essentially a second stage in the process. The exporters, potential or actual, will obviously look for those markets where they can most easily sell their products: in fact those markets with much the same demand conditions as exist at home. Other countries, of course, will be going through the same sort of process, so that trade will tend to be carried out between countries with similar domestic demand conditions, i.e. potential imports of one country will be exactly the same as potential exports. Obviously there are a whole host of factors affecting the structure of demand in any one country, but probably the most important single factor is the average level of income, which in turn is related to the level of economic development. Average incomes would tend to be higher in industrialized countries than in primary producing countries for instance. What all this tells us is that countries will on the whole tend to trade largely with other countries in a similar stage of development where the average income level and hence demand pattern are similar. Thus manufacturing countries will over time tend to trade increasingly with one another.

There was thus in the post-war period an inbuilt advantage for the manufacturing countries if these 'normal' determinants of trade were allowed to operate. In fact the increase in exports of manufactured products was very much greater than that of primary products. Between 1952 and 1964 exports of the former increased at an annual average rate of 9 to 10 per cent compared with an annual average rate of 2½ per cent for the latter. This has long been a general feature of the world system but has been even more pronounced in the post-World War II period. Indeed in this period

[7] S. B. Linder *An Essay in Trade and Transformation* (New York 1961).

world trade in manufactures grew faster than world production of manufactures, indicating a considerable process of international specialization, with beneficial effects on the level of real income and on the rate of economic growth. Similarly the markets of industrial areas grew faster than those of primary producing countries, e.g. the U.S.A. and O.E.C.D. countries grew by 17 per cent and 10 per cent respectively while Latin America and South East Asia grew by $3\frac{1}{2}$ per cent and $4\frac{1}{2}$ per cent respectively.

Apart from this apparently endogenous factor, there were temporary features in the post-war period which indicated that growth of real income and of international trade might well be very rapid. Due to the dislocation to the domestic economies of most countries caused by two world wars and the Great Depression, people had been forced to postpone consumption and build up savings, creating a large, pent-up demand for consumption goods. In conjunction with the more or less full employment attained after the war this pent-up demand led to a tremendous increase in consumer spending which in turn necessitated a corresponding increase in investment to meet the increased demand. This expansion occurred in most countries and was thus self-regulating in the sense that no single country was likely to emerge with an unmanageable trade deficit because of it. Expansion in one country might well lead to an increase in imports but since much the same expansion was occurring elsewhere the increased imports were more or less offset by increased exports. Trade was thus not curtailed more than absolutely necessary, and was as we have seen a most expansionary force in the world economy.

One final factor in the growth of trade must be mentioned – the comparative freedom of world trade. In an attempt to reduce external disequilibrium, countries had in the inter-war and wartime period imposed very stringent controls on trade, such that, by the beginning of the post-war period, trade was virtually completely regulated by government action. Tariffs, quotas, bilateral trading agreements, state trading, etc., all combined to put international trade into a strait-jacket. And however great the potential for trade expansion, unless these restrictions were lifted there was little opportunity for it to become real. However, the sheer uncertainty of unilateral action and Britain's disastrous experience with convertibility in 1947 showed that concerted measures were absolutely essential if the trade barriers were to be lifted. After the failure of the World Trading Organization to get off the ground when America refused to ratify the Havana Charter in 1948 attention was turned to the slightly less intractable solution of regional trade and payments co-operation. For a variety of reasons, economic and non-economic, the weight of American aid was thrown behind the creation of a trading organization in Western Europe. Thus supranational bodies were set up to organize and regulate international trade and payments between the countries of Western Europe. Under the aegis of the Organization for European Economic Co-operation, and the European Payments Union, and with the conditional clauses of Marshall Aid to spur them on, the countries of Western Europe undertook to liberalize trade, initially amongst themselves and then with other countries. Recovery was surprisingly rapid. The natural buoyancy in the world economy and in the individual countries themselves, allied with full employment, led to a period of remarkable growth, until by 1958 the members of O.E.E.C. and E.P.U. felt able to announce full convertibility of their currencies and a fully multilateral trading system. At this point the E.P.U. was wound up and the O.E.E.C. was transformed into the wider but somewhat weaker body O.E.C.D. The importance of these regional bodies cannot be overemphasized as a means to reducing uncertainty among participating members and allowing the expansionary force to emerge.

In this post-war revival of trade, so encouraging to real income in investment and growth, Britain naturally participated. International trade once again becomes a major expansionary force with beneficial effects throughout the economy.

TABLE 34

Growth of Exports in the World Economy, 1870–1964[a]

1870–90	2·6%
1890–1913	2·1%
1913–25	1·9%
1925–38	2·1%
1952–64	4·0%

[a] J. R. Parkinson, 'The Progress of United Kingdom Exports' in D. J. Robertson and L. C. Hunter (eds.) *The British Balance of Payments* (Edinburgh 1966), p. 6.

As a result exports again come to be an important part of the British economy, and as a percentage of G.N.P. increased from 9 per cent in 1939 to 16 per cent in 1968.

However, as exports increased, so did imports. Although the rate varies from year to year, the average was around 5 per cent per annum, which is a high figure by historical standards.

TABLE 35

Growth of Imports into U.K., 1870–1964[a]

1870–90	3·2%
1890–1913	2·1%
1913–25	1.1%
1925–38	0.8%
1952–64	5·0%

[a] G. F. Ray, 'British Imports of Manufactured Goods', *National Institute Economic Review*, March 1960.

The reasons for the increase in imports are precisely those that accounted for the increase in exports. The natural tendency for manufacturing countries to trade with one another, increased specialization resulting from increased trade liberalization, the existence of pent-up demand which was released and stimulated by the full employment policies followed by the government.

Undoubtedly trade, as we saw, was an expansionary force in the post-war economy. However, consideration must now be given to the relative performance of British exports, which as we shall see was somewhat disappointing as compared both with the growth of exports of other, competitor, countries and with the growth of imports, particularly of manufactured goods.

Since the end of the last century Britain's share of world trade has fallen consistently.

TABLE 36

Britain's Percentage Share of World Trade in Manufactured Goods, 1885–1964[a]

1885	37·1	Richardson and Aldcroft
1913	25·4	
1938	22·0	Blackaby
1953	22·0	
1964	14·0	

[a] F. Blackaby, 'British Share of World Trade in Manufactures', *Woolwich Economic Papers*, no. 8, 1965; and D. Aldcroft and H. W. Richardson *The British Economy 1870–1939* (London 1969).

This decrease has been called the 'central fact about the economy, and the most illuminating single set of figures to describe what has happened to the British economy [since the war]'.[8]

[8] Blackaby, op. cit., p. 3.

The British export performance has been especially bad in what were our traditional markets, the Overseas Sterling Area. From 1945 to 1963 our share of the market in O.S.A. fell from 58 per cent to 38 per cent, a decrease of a third, whereas in most other markets the performance has not been so bad, the British share falling from 13 per cent in 1954 to 12 per cent in 1966.

It has been suggested that, as in the inter-war period, the structure of world trade was unfavourable to Britain; that this country was too heavily committed to slow-growing commodities. This is not likely to be a major explanation however, nor should it have been too difficult, if this were the case, for British manufacturers to switch to faster growing products. In fact Britain's share of the market has been reduced in both fast- and slow-growing products. Some other countries, Japan for instance, which had a distribution between fast- and slow-growing products similar to Britain, actually increased their share of the market in both categories, which suggests that the overall distribution cannot have been all that significant.

There may well be other structural features which inhibit faster growth of exports in the long run. H. G. Johnson has shown[9] that when a country engages in trade, given a stable relationship of prices and exchange rates with its partners and conditions of external equilibrium, its rate of growth will be significantly determined by the income elasticity of demand for exports and imports. Other things being equal, that is, the higher the income elasticity of demand for exports and the lower the income elasticity of demand for imports, the greater the rate of growth it is possible to achieve without upsetting the trade balance.[10]

Empirical evidence has shown that for most countries the income elasticities of demand for exports and imports were not too dissimilar, the main exceptions being Japan, U.S.A. and U.K.

The conclusion which can be drawn from this comparison is that if relative prices remain unchanged 'Britain can only grow half as fast as the rest of the world in the long run if it wants to maintain its exchange rate'[11] and also of course external balance. Income elasticity of demand for imports is almost twice as high as that for

[9] H. G. Johnson, 'Increasing Productivity, Income Price Trends and the Trade Balance', *International Trade and Economic Growth* (1958).

[10] Compare this with p. 12. That is, in a period of generally falling income a low elasticity of demand for exports would be favourable, while in a period of generally increasing income, a high elasticity of demand for exports would be the most favourable for the exporting country.

[11] H. S. Houthakker and S. P. Magee, 'Income and Price Elasticities in World Trade', *Review of Economics and Statistics*, vol. 51, 1969.

TABLE 37

Income Elasticity for Imports and Exports of Selected Countries[a]

Imports Income elasticity		Exports Income elasticity
1·66	U.K.	0·86
1·23	Japan	3·55
1·80	Germany	2·08
1·51	U.S.A.	0·99

[a] H. S. Houthakker and S. P. Magee, 'Income and Price Elasticities in World Trade', *Review of Economics and Statistics*, vol. 51, 1969.

exports. This is in complete contrast to Japan, where the income elasticity for exports is almost three times that for imports.

One reason for this discrepancy may be the geographical pattern of exports. British exports are still disproportionately directed towards developing countries, in particular those belonging to the Commonwealth, which have a very active policy of industrialization through import substitution. This has the effect of replacing, on the whole British, exports with domestically produced goods. Britain might be able to offset this sort of disadvantage if her exports were competitive enough, but they are apparently not and it is the combination of uncompetitiveness and unfavourable export pattern that has been the cause of the comparatively disappointing export performance.

As to the fact of uncompetitiveness, there seems to be little doubt. One element is obviously price competitiveness which plays an identifiable though not dominant role in explaining market shares. Empirical evidence shows that between 1953 and 1963 Britain underwent a consistent decline in price competitiveness of about 1·15 per cent per annum. Long-term price elasticities in the world economy tend to be very high so that over time it would be expected that exports would respond to a gradual deterioration of price competitiveness. Junge and Rhomberg found that price changes accounted for between two-fifths and half of the changes in market shares that were observed. However, other countries, such as for instance Germany, show similar price movements and yet maintain and actually increase their share of the market; so that price competitiveness by itself is obviously an incomplete explanation of export performance.

Not only do British export prices increase faster, they tend to be less flexible and responsive to changing conditions than those of their rivals. Thus when world demand increases, price per unit of output remains much the same (apart from long-term changes), whilst supply constraints prevent an increased volume of goods from being exported. On the other hand when demand eases, British export prices do not fall as much as those of other countries. In the machine tool industry for example, firms simply postpone delivery dates when world demand increases. There appears to be little doubt that the refusal of British exporters to tailor their prices to economic conditions abroad has had an adverse effect on export sales.

Closely related to price comparability are those aspects of non-price competition, which become more or less important depending on the competitiveness of prices. These include such things as quality and design of products, delivery dates, after-sales service, etc. It is even more difficult to assess the impact of these factors on exports; but such evidence as does exist suggests that Britain does not fare too badly compared with her main competitors. British goods, however, are not so superior that they can offset the other disadvantages we have noted. It appears from the evidence that as well as being uncompetitive as regards prices, certain British export industries suffer particularly from a shortage of physical capacity. Certainly in the earlier part of the post-war period, up to around 1955, the economy as a whole was subject to obvious physical shortages, though by the late fifties this had ceased to be a general problem. Certain sectors, however, continued to be faced with this difficulty, e.g. chemical and machine tool industries. These shortages led to lengthening delivery dates, which in turn had a very significant impact on the inflow of new orders, and as a determinant of the level of exports, in Britain at least, were a more important factor than price changes.

It is possible to understand how physical shortages could have been important in the early post-war period, but less so towards the end. Obviously a flourishing home market will pre-empt a large proportion of total domestic production, but on the other hand a flourishing home economy is regarded as being essential for success in exporting. In Britain, however, domestic demand has been increasing faster than domestic production, in the Harrod/Domar sense, and the economy has been faced with a situation of almost continuous excess demand.

The almost automatic response of governments to the periodic crises which arose as a result of this excess demand was to impose deflationary measures in the hope that the contraction of the home market would force producers to sell abroad. At best this itself can only be a temporary palliative, external equilibrium only being achieved at the expenses of growth and a full utilization of resources at home. Once the immediate crisis was over and the economy was allowed to expand once more the situation of excess imports would again come to the fore. Thus it is not true to say, as some have done, that the British problem was of a short-term cyclical nature. The problem was endemic, the apparent equilibrium which was achieved periodically was achieved only at the expense of full employment and growth. Only if a structural change occurred, with exports on a permanently higher level and/or imports on a lower level, could equilibrium be said to have been achieved. Indeed it has been persuasively argued[12] that the 'stop-go' policies followed by governments in response to the external situation had a negative impact on growth through their adverse effect on business expectation and domestic investment.

The precise causal relationship between economic growth and exports is still far from clear. It has been maintained that the fact that Britain is least able to hold her share of world markets when demand pressures at home are at their greatest implies that, to some extent at least, exports are limited by availability and hence by the level of domestic activity. In time anything which increases economic growth increases capacity and hence the availability of goods for export. This view was given semi-official sanction in the N.E.D.C. report published in 1964 which stated that 'to some extent the rapid increase in exports [of other countries] was due to the same supply factors that led to the growth in output'.[13] In Britain, on the other hand, for the economy as a whole the shortfall of exports due to slow growth has been estimated as being of the order of £620m.

This presumed relationship must be too simple, however, for as Harrod and Domar show, growth affects both capacity and demand, and only when the former increases faster than the latter does growth lead to an excess of exports over imports. It is also perfectly obvious that the nature of the growth can have a significant effect on the balance of trade. If growth at home was essentially due to increased demand stimulated by inflationary government measures, or due to an increase in investment without accompanying increases in productivity, i.e. capital widening and not capital deepening, then there is every likelihood that imports will be sucked in to meet the excess demand. If growth was, however, due to an increase in

[12] S. Wells, *British Export Performance: A Comparative Study* (Cambridge 1963), p. 67.

[13] National Economic Development Council *Export Trends* (H.M.S.O., London 1963), p. 14.

productivity, the increase in capacity is quite likely to be greater than the increase in demand stimulated by the improvement. There is less likely to be balance of trade problems and less likely to be any forced inhibitions on growth. Thus government policy by creating uncertainty and reducing investment may well have prevented potential productivity increases from being realized and made it more likely that in periods of future growth demand would increase faster than capacity with consequent adverse effects on the balance of trade.

Equally discouraging has been the British import performance, especially with regard to imports of manufactured goods. When imports of all goods grew at an annual average rate of 4 per cent per annum, imports of manufactured goods increased by 15 per cent per annum. Thus, whereas in 1955 imports of manufactured goods accounted for 25 per cent of all imports, by 1965 they had risen to 44 per cent of the total, and grew twice as fast as domestic production of manufactured goods. To some extent this was a normal feature of international specialization which occurred in all industrialized countries following trade liberalization, e.g. paper, paper board, chemicals, machine tools. But in Britain certain features made the situation more dangerous than elsewhere. One was the comparatively poor export performance, which left less leeway for large imports. Another was the fact that Britain's imports of food and raw materials were much larger than other countries', again reducing the amount of leeway available for imports of manufactured products. Thirdly, our international financial commitments meant that Britain required a larger surplus than most other countries. Finally, as we have noted above, the figures were as low as they were because the government was often forced to cut back on the level of domestic activity. There is little doubt that if the economy had been allowed to grow constantly at full employment level the import level would be even higher. (Exports would also be higher; what the net balance would be is impossible to say, of course.)

Despite the evidence of high price elasticity for imports of −5, price competition does not appear to have been the dominant factor in explaining this phenomenon. Especially is this true for high quality precision goods where such characteristics as performance, design, etc., outweigh quite large differences in price. There is always a trade-off, of course, between lower price and better performance, but the price differential must often be very large indeed before firms go for inferior but cheaper commodities.[14]

[14] Private conversation with industrialists in North Lancashire in February

As far as can be made out, the most important single influence on the level of imports has been the rate of domestic absorption in Britain. Normally excess imports are kept in check by holding down the level of economic activity. However, as the economy periodically builds up steam and growth quickens, domestic demand exceeds domestic supply and the difference is made up via increased imports.

TABLE 38

Growth of United Kingdom Exports and Imports[a]

	Growth rate	Av. increase in exports	Av. increase in imports
Expansion periods (1935–55, 1958–60, 1962–4)	5·8%	4·9%	7·9%
Stagnation periods (1955–8, 1960–2, 1964–6)	0·9%	2·7%	1·3%

[a] W. A. Eltis, 'Economic Growth and the British Balance of Payments', *District Bank Review*, December 1967.

As the domestic economy booms, exports increase (at a higher rate than in periods of stagnation), but unfortunately imports increase even more quickly, giving an unmanageable trade deficit. Prices increase less in periods of expansion than in stagnation, so there is little doubt that the effective cause of the excessive amount of imports is lack of capacity at home, when in periods of growth demand grows more rapidly than capacity. This lack of capacity seems a valid explanation for the behaviour of the economy as a whole and also for the performance of certain identifiable individual industries, e.g. chemicals, paper and paper board, man-made fibres, steel, domestic appliances and machine tools, where investment has not been adequate to meet demand in the periods of full employment and rapid growth.

ADDITIONAL READING

R. E. BALDWIN 'The Commodity Composition of Trade: Selected Industrial Countries, 1900–54' (*Rev. of Econs. and Statistics*, 40, 1958)

R. J. BALL *et al.* 'The Relationship Between U.K. Export Performances in Manufactures and International Pressure of Demand' (*Economic Journal*, vol. 76, 1966)

T. BARNA 'Fast and Slow Growing Products in World Trade' (*Nat. Instit. Econ. Rev.*, August 1963)

1969 showed their buying of capital equipment hardly affected by the devaluation of 1967 due to the alleged superior quality of German and Italian alternatives.

H. B. JUNG AND R. R. RHOMBERG 'Prices and Export Performance of Industrial Countries, 1953–63' (*International Monetary and Staff Papers*, vol. 12, 1965)
C. P. KINDLEBERGER 'Foreign Trade and Growth: Lessons from British Experience since 1913' (*Lloyds Bank Review*, July 1962)
A. MAIZELS 'World Trade Trends' (*Woolwich Economic Papers* 7, 1965)
R. MAJOR 'World Trade in Manufactures' (*Nat. Instit. Econ. Rev.*, July 1960)
NATIONAL ECONOMIC DEVELOPMENT COUNCIL *Imported Manufactures: An Inquiry into Competitiveness* (1965)
G. L. REES *Britain and the Post-War European Payments System* (Cardiff 1963)
W. W. ROSTOW *The Economics of Takeoff into Sustained Growth* (1963)
M. F. SCOTT *A Study of United Kingdom Imports* (Cambridge 1963)

CHAPTER 7

The Balance of Payments and Growth

Throughout most of the nineteenth century, Britain imported more from abroad than she exported. The trade deficit was, however, more than offset by surplus on other items in the balance of payments which gave her a net surplus. Britain was able to export her net earnings in the form of capital, and emerged as by far the most important foreign lender in the world. These invisible earnings consisted of payments rendered for the financial and other services of the City of London, credits from shipping and income from overseas assets. It was this last item which increased most rapidly, dominating the invisible account by the outbreak of World War I. By 1913 net income from invisibles was sufficient to pay for over one-half the cost of imported goods, and net income from overseas assets alone paid for 30 per cent of net imports.

	City Earnings	*Shipping*	*Net Income from Abroad*	*£m. Exports*	*Imports*	*Trade[1] Balance*
1910–13	+78	+99	+183	474	611	−137

Thus at the beginning of the twentieth century Britain still enjoyed a clear supremacy in the international economy. Her exports amounted to 13 per cent of the world total, imports to 15 per cent and her shipping to 40 per cent of world shipping. As a result of this prominence sterling became the most important currency after gold, mainly for use as a key currency but also partly as an international reserve currency; and finally, Britain became the leading international banker.

The late nineteenth century was a period of comparative stability in international economic relations, and Britain utilized this stability to enhance her economic position. World trade was increasing the scope and benefit of international specialization. This in turn

[1] A. E. Holmans, 'Invisible Earnings' in D. J. Robertson and L. C. Hunter (eds) *The British Balance of Payments* (Edinburgh 1966), p. 45.

necessitated finance, both long and short term, and Britain with her sophisticated financial institutions was able to meet this world-wide demand for capital. It is a moot point whether in the long run such finance would have been better invested at home.[2] However, it was obviously profitable for the City to lend abroad and this is what did happen. Because of the dominant role of a single (and free trade) country, the international financial system, the Gold Standard, was able to grow and adapt to the needs of the international economy. This meant that Britain, though a large foreign lender, could economize on her holdings of reserves, often as low as £50m., and lend the remainder of her net surplus abroad. Britain was so successful at exploiting this system that by 1914 her foreign assets amounted to £400m. and both net foreign lending and net foreign receipts were running at around £200m. per annum.

Britain was never in any serious balance of payments difficulties during the pre-war period. It was the First World War which brought this state of affairs abruptly to an end, though it is quite possible to argue that the economic development of other countries, already threatening Britain's primacy before 1914, would eventually have put a strain on the commercial and financial operations through which a healthy balance of payments was maintained.

It was, however, clearly the effect of the war itself which brought the sudden weakening of the balance of trade, when the deficit increased from an average of £150m. in 1910–13 to an average of £342m. throughout the 1920s. Thus unless Britain were to reduce her international commitments, in particular to reduce foreign lending, or compensate for the enlarged trade deficit by enlarged surpluses elsewhere, internal expansion would have to be curtailed in order to maintain external equilibrium. This problem was accentuated by the fact that Britain, to pay for the war, had liquidated between £850m. and £1,000m. of her foreign capital assets, or between 20 and 25 per cent of her total holdings.

Despite the dislocation caused by the war, however, Britain soon embarked on a renewed burst of foreign lending. By 1920 the earnings on foreign investment amounted to £200m. per annum, and by 1925 to £250m. per annum. Although the latter yield was higher than the pre-war figure, in real terms it was still far less. The inflow amounted to 6 per cent of G.N.P. compared with 9½ per cent before the war, and paid for 20 per cent of imports as compared with 26 per cent. Even these figures understate the diminished importance

[2] See for instance: A. K. Cairncross *Home and Foreign Investment 1870–1913* (Cambridge 1953), p. 187.

of foreign earnings in the economy, for whereas prior to 1914 their contribution had been made in conditions of boom, during the 1920s the relative size of interest payments was increased by the under-employment of productive resources at home.

Moreover, Britain was now lending far beyond her capacity. Throughout the 1920s new overseas issues averaged around £125m. per annum. To some extent this foreign lending did serve the useful purpose of easing the problem of reconstruction in some foreign countries. On the whole, however, its impact on the economy was adverse. It seems likely that the foreign investment was undertaken at the expense of home investment, and was partly responsible for the failure of British industries to participate in the long expansionary upswing of the world economy in the 1920s. Britain's trading account was adversely affected. That an external deficit did not emerge was almost certainly due to the fact that the authorities were forced to introduce deflationary and hence growth-inhibiting measures to maintain external equilibrium. One indication of the impact of deflation, apart from the fact that unemployment was continuously above 10 per cent, was the fact that domestic investment as a percentage of G.N.P. fell from 4 per cent in 1913 to 3 per cent in 1925.

The weakness in the balance of payments meant that Britain's reserves of gold never exceeded £172 million throughout the decade. Though this was larger than her holdings during the heyday of the Gold Standard, conditions were vastly different. In real terms they were of course far less, while in the 1920s the external position was far less buoyant and stable than it was in the latter part of the nineteenth century. The need to cushion speculative flights of capital was therefore much greater. As was to be shown in 1931, Britain's gold reserves were simply not adequate to meet the demands put on them.

By the 1920s the increase in the volume of world trade was outstripping the supplies of gold coming on to the world markets. While there is no 'correct' ratio of gold to trade, it was nevertheless thought that reserves were inadequate, and that unless they could somehow be augmented the growth of world trade would be inhibited, with deflationary consequences throughout the world economy. Following the Genoa Conference of 1922 many countries began to hold sterling and dollars as reserves to economize on the use of gold. By this time the dollar was the strongest of all national currencies and was an obvious candidate for this function. The pound also became accepted as a reserve currency largely because of its historical importance, even though by then the British economy was relatively much weaker. The resulting addition to the foreign sterling debt added a further element of instability to the system.

To induce foreign countries to hold sterling, Britain had to build up her foreign reserves. This she did by borrowing short, thus adding further to her foreign debts. By 1928 her short-term liabilities were of the order of £500m. gross and £200m. net. In a period of complete stability this might well have been acceptable, but in the conditions of the 1920s it was storing up trouble.

Britain was in fact trying to do the impossible. Given her small[3] current account surplus she could perhaps have built up her gold reserves and eventually restored confidence, or she could have lent abroad without having to borrow short. She tried to do both. The effect was to put intolerable pressure on the balance of payments which in turn hindered growth.

The concurrent instability of the world economy added to Britain's troubles. Two new factors came into play in the game of international finance after 1918. The first was reparations and war debt; the second, the emergence of the U.S.A. as the leading creditor nation. The latter circumstance was partly a corollary of the former, since Germany and other nations owing money as a result of the war and the peace treaties borrowed heavily from the U.S.A. to meet their obligations. Although America lent enormous amounts abroad, however, she failed to provide the impetus to trade which Britain had managed to do in the nineteenth century. She imposed high tariffs on imports making it difficult or impossible for debtors to service their debt except by further and more hazardous borrowing. She gave short-term loans rather than long-term. She lent to foreign governments, rather than directly to industrialists or merchants.

So long as the U.S.A. was prepared to lend abroad there was no great danger, but should a time come when America either could not or would not offer further credit support the whole edifice would come tumbling down. Such a situation did in fact occur after the Great Crash of 1929, although there had been intimations of a rundown prior to this. The Great Crash had a disastrous effect on America's foreign lending which fell by about 60 per cent between 1927–9 and 1932–3. Borrowers were forced to default on their obligations, and capital flows which, on the whole, were of a stabilizing nature under the automatic Gold Standard now turned perverse as countries fought to hold their exchange rates (usually unsuccess-

[3] In real terms only one-third to one-half of the pre-war level after adjusting for price changes.

fully). In the currency crises of 1931 Britain's economic difficulties came to a head with revolutionary effect on international monetary policy.

In the 1930s the British situation changed somewhat. Despite the imposition of stringent tariffs and quotas, the trade deficit remained as large as ever, averaging out at about £340m. per annum. While the volume of exports was reduced, that of imports actually increased: Britain's share of world imports rose from 15·5 per cent in the late 1920s to 17·5 per cent in the late 1930s. That this did not lead to an even greater deficit was due entirely to the terms of trade which moved very much in Britain's favour (see Chapter 6).

Meanwhile the net inflow of invisible earnings also fell, from £480m. in 1927–9 to £280m. in 1933–5, though there was a subsequent increase to £355m. in 1936–8. Even so, income from this source was at least £100m. down on the figure for the 1920s. The combined effect of the continuing large trade deficit, and worsening of the invisible account, turned the current account from a surplus of around £109m. per annum in the 1920s (with one year of deficit in 1926) to an average deficit of £96m. per annum in the 1930s.

In the conditions prevailing after 1931, however, an imbalance of this kind no longer had a seriously inhibiting effect on growth. Britain took action to reduce the pressure on other areas of the account; in particular she took steps to reduce foreign lending. Immediately after the abandonment of the Gold Standard in 1931, an embargo was placed on foreign investment, the effect of which was enhanced by the lack of confidence and the uncertainty in the international situation. The upswing of economic activity at home also had the effect of reducing the comparative attractiveness of foreign lending. The position is summarized as follows.

TABLE 39

Home and Foreign Investment 1925–36[a]

£m.

	Domestic investment	Foreign investment
1925–9	165	115 (Empire 67)
1932–6	124	31 (Empire 28)

[a] A. Youngson *Britain's Economic Growth 1920–1966* (1967), p. 124.

The reduction in foreign lending did not end the repayments of foreign debtors, so that in 1932, 1935, 1936 and 1938 there was net foreign disinvestment. Finally the abandonment of the Gold

Standard and the depreciation of sterling meant that, at least for a while, Britain appeared to be the safest repository of speculative funds. Funds which had left London during the 1931 crisis now returned, even though interest rates were low, attracted by political and economic stability. Partly as a result of this short-term inflow, gold reserves increased from £191m. in 1931 to £835m. in 1938.

Meanwhile the role of sterling in the world economy was perceptibly altered. With the creation of the Sterling Area in 1932, sterling became a regional as opposed to an international currency. Sterling countries held up to 60 per cent of Britain's total net liabilities, and as a group these were in surplus for most of the period, so that the pressure on sterling was very much reduced. There was unlikely to be a great or sudden selling of sterling which would inhibit expansionary policies by the government. To a large extent domestic policy was immune to the vicissitudes of the external sector which was thus not the constraint on growth it had been in the 1920s. The balance of payments position for the decade is summarized in Table 40.

Even though during most of the decade the external account did not cause alarm, there were disquieting signs that towards the end of the 1930s the position was worsening. This deterioration was of course made worse after 1938 by the beginning of war preparations. Short-term capital movements had resumed a speculative character and were moving out of London in great quantities. Gold reserves decreased from £835m. to £450m. at the outbreak of war. Despite a slowing down in the pace of economic recovery the trade deficit in 1937 was the largest in the country's history and the income from invisibles fell from a peak of £386m. in 1937 to £322m. in 1938. However, before the external situation had time to bite, Britain entered World War II and attention was diverted to more immediate matters.

During the war Britain paid scant attention to the long-term prospect of her balance of payments. She sold over £1,000m. of foreign capital assets yielding, by Keynes' estimation, an annual inflow of £100m. The external debt was meanwhile increased by almost £3,000m. which, added to the £5,000m. outstanding, swelled her sterling liabilities to £8,500m. Britain also ran down her gold reserves by £150m. so that the net external position was estimated to have worsened by at least £4,200m. The ratio of assets to liabilities worsened considerably and helped to keep the economy on a precarious knife-edge throughout the post-war period.

As we have already seen, the British export performance in the

TABLE 40

Fluctuations in the Balance of Payments 1930–8[a]

(+ = receipts; − = payments)

	Adverse balance of trade (1)	Net invisible exports (2)	Balance of payments on current account (3)	Income from overseas investment (4)
1930	−282	+310	+28	+209
1931	−323	+218	−104	+169
1932	−217	+166	−51	+156
1933	−196	+196	0	+150
1934	−221	+214	−7	+159
1935	−185	+217	+32	+172
1936	−260	+241	−18	+184
1937	−339	+283	−56	+198
1938	−284	+230	−54	+185

	New overseas issues (5)	Net inflow of long-term capital (6)
1930	−98	−19
1931	−41	+1
1932	−37	+21
1933	−83	−6
1934	−63	−36
1935	−51	−40
1936	−61	−126
1937	−60	+11
1938	−29	+40

	Short-term capital movements (7)	Sterling balances in London (8)
1930	+17	
1931	−99	411
1932	−100	468
1933	+179	538
1934	+26	580
1935	−54	600
1936	+129	721
1937	+12	808
1938	−137	598

[a] H. W. Richardson *Economic Recovery in Britain 1932–39* (1967), p. 58–9.

post-war period was good. Earnings increased at an annual average rate of 4·5 per cent, so that whereas in 1938 exports only paid for

64 per cent of total imports, by 1968–9 they paid for 94 per cent of the total. On the other hand the relative value of the invisible earnings fell sharply. In the past, the British trade deficit had been more than offset by the surplus in the invisible account. In the post-war period the invisible account, though always in surplus, was not strong enough to offset weakness elsewhere in the economy. As Table 41 shows, the invisible surplus becomes gradually smaller up to the mid 1960s and has been estimated to have declined at an average rate of 8·3 per cent, though there was some improvement towards the end of the decade.

TABLE 41

Summary of Invisible Imports and Exports[a] *1952–69 (net) £m.*

(+ = receipts; − = payments)

	1952	1955	1960	1965	1967	1969
Government	−61	−138	−282	−446	−449	−467
Shipping	+134	−30	−34	+2	+69	−20
Travel	−3	−14	−17	−97	−38	+35
Interest profits and dividends	+252	+174	+240	+447	+368	+832
Civil aviation	0	−3	+18	+23	+23	+41
Other services	+122	+171	+222	+276	+396	+546
Private transactions	−2	−2	+3	−52	−43	−55
Invisible balance	+444	+158	+150	+153	+252	+581
Visible balance	−279	−313	−408	−281	−632	−184

[a] F. N. Burton and P. Galambos 'The Role of Invisible Trade in the United Kingdom Balance of Payments 1952–1966', *National Provincial Bank Review*, May 1968, p. 11; and Central Statistical Office *United Kingdom Balance of Payments 1971* (H.M.S.O., London 1971), pp. 16–20.

If we exclude the government sector, the invisible surplus jumps very sharply by over £400m. by the end of the period, although even so the private account paid for only 40 per cent of what it did before the war. Table 42 gives the growth rates of the main items.

Thus whereas the government's account is now a major item in the invisible trade sector compared with the inter-war period, it can be seen that both private and official invisible receipts and expenditures have grown at much the same rate.

We can now look briefly at the individual items which make up the invisible account. Undoubtedly the most disappointing has been the shipping item. Shipping has traditionally earned a large surplus, reflecting Britain's pre-eminent position as international carrier, but since the war it has recorded a deficit in the two periods 1955–6

TABLE 42

Growth of Invisibles and Imports since 1938

1938 = 100[a]

	Merchandise imports	Total invisibles		Private invisibles	
		Payment	Receipts	Payment	Receipts
1938	100	100	100	100	100
1946	126	541	211	308	174
1950	275	548	330	509	327
1955	403	850	417	797	397
1960	492	1,095	524	1,017	520
1966	626	1,502	698	1,364	696
1967	675	1,557	729	1,436	727
1969	856	1,938	967	1,849	975

[a] M. Panic, 'Britain's Invisible Balance', *Lloyds Bank Review*, July 1968, p. 15; and Central Statistical Office, op. cit., p. 13.

and 1960–4. Although there has been some subsequent improvement, the ratio of receipts to payments has declined disastrously. Between 1952 and 1961, gross overseas earnings from shipping increased by 314 per cent in Germany, 281 per cent in Japan and 113 per cent in Italy, but by only 11 per cent in Britain, though again there was a slight improvement by the end of the period.

For civil aviation, the other item in the transport account, apart from 1955–7, receipts have been constantly in excess of payments. But though in absolute terms the surplus of 1967 was five times that of 1952, the figures do show that the percentage excess of receipts over payments has been falling continuously since the peak of 1959. The travel item shows a continuous deficit up till 1968 despite the fact that Britain is a major exporter of travel services.

By far the most profitable item of invisible trade is 'interest, profit and dividends'. By 1968 this amounted to just over £300m. (which was by normal standards quite low). While many of Britain's assets were liquidated during the war, they were quickly made up again and by 1947 net earnings were greater than they were in 1938. The increase in assets would have given an even larger surplus had it not been that, since the war, payments had risen even more rapidly. Before the war payments on this account were quite negligible, but their subsequent rise has resulted from foreign, and in particular American, investment in Britain. Payments grew much faster than receipts and in 1966, for the first time, the surplus failed to increase.

The sub-group 'other services' is a somewhat mixed one, including such items as insurance, banking services, royalties, etc., for which

TABLE 43

Interest Profits and Dividends: Payments and Receipts 1938–67

	Payments	Receipts	1938 = 100 Net balance
1938	100	100	100
1946–50	349	151	113
1951–5	732	227	130
1956–60	1,027	277	133
1961–7	1,351	378	191

precise information is not available. One of the main elements is what is called the City's earnings, and while there are no official figures it was estimated in 1963 that these amounted to a net surplus of between £120m. and £185m. Most of the other services listed under this heading show a net deficit.

In summary, we can say that private invisible earnings have diminished in relative importance in Britain's balance of payments accounts since the war. While they yielded a net surplus large enough to pay for 30 per cent of the nation's imports in 1914–38, by the 1950s this surplus paid for only 13 per cent of the total and by 1968 for only 11 per cent.

The final item in the invisible account is that of government transactions. This has been in chronic and ever-increasing deficit since 1945, which of course reduces still further the ability of the invisible account earnings as a whole to offset any imbalance of trade. Figures since 1952 are given in Table 44 and show that by the 1960s the government deficit was absorbing up to 80 per cent of the net private invisible surplus. In the inter-war period in contrast the government account was quite negligible.

TABLE 44

Government Total Current Payments and Receipts[a]

	Payments	Receipts	£m. Net balance
1952	219	165	−54
1955	243	105	−128
1960	327	45	−282
1965	492	46	−446
1969	515	48	−467

[a] Central Statistical Office, op. cit., p. 14.

The main items in this category are military expenditures overseas, economic grants and subscriptions or contributions to international organizations. Not all of this expenditure is, even in directly economic terms, 'wasted', for some of the military expenditures comes back to Britain in the form of imports of goods and services, allowing for which it has been estimated that the deficit on military expenditures should be adjusted downwards by 20 per cent.

Looking then at the post-war balance of payments situation as a whole, we can suggest the following, simplified, argument. The balance of trade deficit has been relatively reduced since the inter-war years, but the surplus from invisible trade has fallen even more rapidly. In consequence Britain has suffered recurrent balance of payments problems, with adverse effect on her economic growth.

Two components of the balance of payments account, however, still await consideration: the long- and short-term capital transactions. Despite the widespread, and apparently authoritative assumption to the contrary,[4] Britain did not emerge from the Second World War having liquidated all her long-term foreign assets. As we said earlier, Keynes estimated that Britain in fact sold about £1,000m. of her total assets of just under £3,000m. by 1945, and made further sales of £500m. in the immediate post-war period, still leaving intact long-term assets abroad to the value of around £1,500m. Net indebtedness was estimated to be very small in those early post-war years and was very soon made up by further foreign investment at a level unprecedented in absolute terms in British history. By the end of 1967 British long-term foreign assets amounted to £12,600m., of which £11,500m. were private assets. It follows that since the war total foreign investment must have been of the order of £9,000m. and even this might be something of an undervaluation. Britain made the transition from being a net debtor to being a net creditor in the early 1950s and has remained one ever since.

Even though the overall position remained fairly straightforward, there were some changes in the pattern of long-term capital flows which affected the position of sterling in the world economy. Traditionally British foreign investment had been of the fixed assets and debenture type, such as continued well into the 1920s. Since the Second World War a change in distribution has occurred. Of the three different types of long-term lending, fixed debt, direct private investment and official capital flows, the first, once predominant, has been far less important recently, and there has been a net liquidation of portfolio holdings.

The new outlays have been mainly in the form of direct investment and government grants and loans (which includes aid). Direct

[4] E.g. H. Macmillan *Winds of Change 1914–1939* (1966), p. 18.

TABLE 45

United Kingdom Long-Term Capital Outlays 1958–66[a]

(– = outflow)

	1958	1959	1960	1961	1962	1963	1964	1965	1966
Government grants and loans	–113	–190	–175	–173	–200	–216	–250	–228	–219
Private long-term capital									
Direct	–144	–196	–250	–226	–209	–236	–263	–318	–314
Oil			–109	–115	–72	–79	–136	–131	–115
Portfolio	–166	–107	37	28	39	–14	–7	91	112

[a] R. N. Cooper, 'The Balance of Payments', in R. Caves (ed.) *Britain's Economic Prospects* (1968), p. 173.

investment, mainly by overseas subsidiaries of British firms, has by now become the largest single category and accounts for about 80 per cent of the total private overseas investment, though it still forms only 48 per cent of the stock of overseas holdings. Of such industrial investment about half has been directed to the Sterling Area, in particular to the economically developed, fast-growing countries, Australia, New Zealand and South Africa. This concentration on direct as opposed to portfolio investment and on the fast-growing countries augmented by large investments in Western Europe in recent years had a rapid and beneficial effect on the invisible account.

While Britain herself has been building up a new range of overseas investments, long-term foreign involvement in this country has also been increasing.

TABLE 46

Long-Term Capital Inflow 1958–68[a]

£m.

	1958	1959	1960	1961	1962	1963	1964	1965	1966	1968
Direct	87	146	135	236	136	160	162	189	224	283
Oil and Miscellaneous	77	26	55	75	57	91	25	65	107	245
Portfolio			43	115	61	78	–34	–46	–49	35

[a] Central Statistical Office, op. cit., p. 26.

As a proportion of Britain's holdings abroad it amounted to 10 per cent in 1912 and to 80 per cent by 1963. By 1967 total long-term liabilities were of the order of £5,000m. of which about 80 per cent was of American origin and tended to be directed towards the fastest growing sectors of the economy such as office equipment, washing machines, agricultural tractors, etc.

TABLE 47

United Kingdom Long-Term External Assets and Liabilities 1962–7

£m.

	Assets		Liabilities	
	1962	1967	1962	1967
Official	709	1,059	2,650	2,887
Private portfolio	3,000	4,159	1,050	1,450
Direct investment (Not oil or banking)	3,400	5,300	1,430	2,350
Other	1,485	2,100	705	1,165
Total long-term private	7,885	11,500	3,185	4,965
Total long-term	8,594	12,609	5,835	7,852

[a] A. G. Kemp, 'Long Term Capital Movements', in Robertson and Hunter, op. cit., p. 149.

As with other categories in the balance of payments accounts the significance of Britain's own investment can be analysed by reference to the immediate effect on the balance of payments and to the indirect effect on resource allocation within the economy.

In a strictly static balance of payments account foreign investment can be shown to benefit the total balance, since on the whole the inflow of dividends, etc., resulting from such foreign investment greatly exceeds the outflow on long-term capital account, and a reduction in one would undoubtedly lead to a reduction in the other. This, however, does not enable us to say whether any particular piece of investment is justified or not.

A measure of the efficiency of resource allocation might involve a comparison of the rate of return on home and foreign investment. The evidence suggests that the rate of return on foreign investment (excluding oil) between 1955 and 1965 averaged out at about 8·7 per cent, while home investment showed an average rate of return of 8·5 per cent in the same period (both yields, however, being much below the 13 per cent for oil). These yields are both post-tax, but since in the case of foreign investment tax receipts accrue to the foreign government, and in the case of domestic investment, to Britain, the social, as opposed to the private, rate of return is likely to be lower on foreign than on domestic investment. Thus a straightforward comparison of the rate of return tends to overstate the benefits obtained from foreign investment.

In addition, a direct comparison of the rate of return shows that British foreign investment tends to be somewhat more inefficient than that of some of its main competitors, in particular the U.S.A. An analysis of the rate of return on foreign investment by U.K. and U.S.A. companies shows that in only one sector, mining, was the rate of return to British companies higher. It has been estimated that on average American investment was 26 per cent more profitable than British foreign investment.

TABLE 48

Comparative Rates of Return on U.K. and U.S.A. Direct Foreign Investment for Selected Years[a]

	1960		1962		1965	
	U.K.	U.S.A.	U.K.	U.S.A.	U.K.	U.S.A.
Agriculture	9·4	(1)	9·6	(1)	8·2	(1)
Mining	19·8	13·1	12·2	11·5	16·7	12·1
Petrol	10·6	11·7	11·4	13·6	11·0	12·7
Manufacture	8·0	10·5	8·2	9·9	8·4	10·4
Trade	7·2	(1)	5·0	(1)	6·6	(1)
Other	3·4	9·4	3·2	9·8	4·3	9·3
Total	9·2	10·8	9·9	11·3	9·2	11·1

(1) Included in 'Other'.

[a] J. Dunning, 'U.K. and U.S. Investment Abroad', *National Provincial Bank Review*, August 1968, p. 13.

A further study of foreign investment in Canada shows that the rate of return on British foreign investment is again lower than that of American, and also of all other countries taken as a group. The conclusion was that 'British investors obtained a return of little more than one-half of that obtained by investors from the United States and from other countries'.[5] One reason given for this disparity is that British firms do not make the effort to seek out the high growth sectors, but are content to maintain traditional, and presumably inefficient, investment patterns.

In general, however, a simple comparison of rates of return on home and foreign investment is an inadequate measure of their efficiency – there are other considerations to be noted. The most authoritative study on this subject[6] suggests that the net effect of a

[5] O. J. Firestone, 'British Investment in Canada', *Westminster Bank Review*, November 1967, p. 31.

[6] W. B. Reddaway *Effects of United Kingdom Direct Investment Overseas*, Interim Report (Cambridge 1967), and Final Report 1970.

marginal increment of foreign investment in increasing exports is rather small. The Reddaway Report, making some assumptions as to alternative positions (assumptions which have been seriously queried by some economists)[7] concluded that the net effect of increasing foreign investment by £100 was to increase the export of capital goods by £9 and other goods by £1½. The slightness of this increase suggests that the main effect of foreign investment is to stimulate domestic production in the receiving country, which replaces the original British exports. This generalization is obviously more applicable to the manufacturing sector, however, than it is to, say, distribution. On the other hand foreign investment is quite likely to be of positive value to the lending country if it has the effect of reducing import prices. Since a great deal of British imports is of food and raw materials, British investment in primary producing sectors, in Canada, for instance, might well provide great benefit in the form of cheap raw materials.

Even if the export of capital was shown to be economically undesirable in itself, however, it would not necessarily be wise as a policy to restrict it. The flow of international capital is very much affected by the state of confidence and stability of international money markets. If one important country, like Britain, were unilaterally to reduce foreign investment by official action, whether for economic reasons or not, this could well reduce the inflow of capital into Britain. The export performance of foreign subsidiaries, particularly of American firms, is better than the average for all industrial firms and their share of total exports is increasing. Thus any precipitate action by Britain to curb the outflow of long-term funds might also reduce the inflow, and Britain might lose more than she gains.

One last question which must be considered in assessing the impact of foreign investment is whether it has any significant effect on the level of domestic investment: that is, whether an increase in one will mean a decrease in the other. Although it is virtually impossible to establish a precise relationship here, most of the evidence suggests that, in the period since World War II at least, foreign investment does not necessarily reduce home investment below what it otherwise would have been.

The second main item in the long-term capital account is that of official capital movements. By the end of our period these amounted to around £200m., and though most of these funds are not allocated

[7] E.g. W. A. Manser, 'Professor Reddaway's Last Word?', *National Westminster Bank Review*, February 1969.

in response to economic considerations they do have an economic impact. The largest single government expenditure overseas is that of aid. The raw figures might, however, lead to an exaggerated estimate of its impact on the economy in the long run. Aid, like private investment, yields a continuous flow of interest payments back to the lending country. Moreover, it has been calculated that aid provides an increase of exports worth about 50 per cent of its total value in any one year.

We have now examined each of the principal elements in the balance of payments accounts. But no discussion of this subject would be complete without some consideration of the role of sterling in the international financial system, and its implications for Britain's external economic position.

Despite the fact that sterling has been a key, and to a lesser extent a reserve, currency since the inter-war period, the massive build-up of overseas holdings of sterling occurred as a result of the need to pay for the war. Net sterling balances increased from £500m. to £3,500m. in 1939–45, and during the post-war period the sum has varied from £3,100m. to £3,800m. By the end of the period the figures were as follows.

TABLE 49

U.K. Short-Term Assets and Liabilities[a]

(+ = increase in assets; – = increase in liabilities)

£m.

	End 1962	1964	1966	1967
Assets:				
Official*	1,362	1,272	1,287	1,123
Private	2,106	3,006	4,513	5,979
Liabilities:				
Official	2,527	2,835	2,929	3,566
Private	2,731	3,690	4,972	6,282
Net:				
Official	–1,165	–1,563	–1,642	–2,443
Private	–625	–683	–459	–303
Total	–1,790	–2,147	–2,101	–2,746
* Of which gold reserves	1,002	827	1,107	1,123

[a] 'An Inventory of U.K. External Assets and Liabilities: end 1967', *Bank of England Quarterly Bulletin*, vol. 8, no. 3, September 1968, p. 276.

A comparison of long-term capital holdings shows that net long-term assets are considerably greater than liabilities, though the Bank of England considers these calculations to be of limited practical significance. What is of importance is the deficit in the short run balance, because it is short-term credit which is the volatile element in the account and which often aggravates a situation of external disequilibrium.

Sterling plays two quite distinct roles in the international economy. It is held by foreign institutions both as a reserve currency and as a key currency. It is very much a moot point whether one function can successfully be maintained without the other. However, a rough distinction between the two must be made. As a reserve currency sterling is held by foreign governments as a backing for the domestic currency and for sundry other reasons. Of the total overseas holdings of sterling in 1965 the amount held by foreign Central Banks was just over £2,000m., of which £1,780m. was held by banks of Sterling Area countries. This part of the Sterling debt is believed not to be very volatile; indeed in times of crises foreign governments may well maintain their holdings rather than rock the international monetary system through putting too much pressure on Great Britain.

The residue of holdings by private institutions and banks amounts to £1,800m. and is held to finance the flow of international trade. This is the key currency element of sterling holdings. Private institutions feel no obligation to prop up a precarious balance of payments position, and through the process known as 'leads and lags' may well bring great pressure on Great Britain when there is the fear of a possible devaluation. Furthermore, for a variety of reasons it is always possible that member countries of the Sterling Area will wish to relinquish their ties and transfer their holdings into gold, as for instance Burma did in 1966. The instability which any such large-scale defections might impart to the whole world currency system led to the Basle Agreement of 1968, which guarantees that such withdrawals of sterling reserves would be automatically replenished.

How do these overseas holdings affect the general external position of the British economy? It has been suggested that the pooling of all the Sterling Area's gold reserves in London economizes on the use of gold by the offsetting seasonal nature of the deficits of some of the Commonwealth countries. This allows the productive resources of the economy to be more fully utilized, either by giving a slight expansionary fillip to the economy or by enabling Britain to lend abroad.

Secondly, as far as the U.K. economy is concerned the level of its resources is affected not only by its own payments relationships, but also by the aggregate net deficit or surplus of the rest of the

Sterling Area with the rest of the world. It appears that both accounts are gradually moving in Britain's disfavour. In the early 1950s Britain's current deficit was offset by the current surplus of the other Sterling Area countries (O.S.A.), but since the 1950s the O.S.A. has run into an aggregate net deficit which appears to be worsening.

TABLE 50

Current Transactions with Non-Sterling Countries[a]

(+ = receipts; − = payments)

£m.

	U.K.	O.S.A.	Total
1950–4 (av.)	−175	194	19
1955–9 (av.)	−147	−61	−208
1960	−626	−395	−1,021
1964	−513	−530	−1,043

[a] A. R. Conan *The Problem of Sterling* (1966), p. 89.

This growing imbalance suggests a structural change in the Sterling Area system which will tend to have a depressant effect on the level of gold reserves, and will worsen Britain's own position.

Meanwhile the offsetting trade patterns which during the 1950s had the effect of economizing on reserves have now given way to a far less complementary pattern, in that the visible surpluses and deficits of both Britain and the O.S.A. are seen to fluctuate together. The reason for this is probably the decline in the relative importance of trade between Britain and the O.S.A. and the exposure of both of them to world influences which have a similar impact on their net balance.

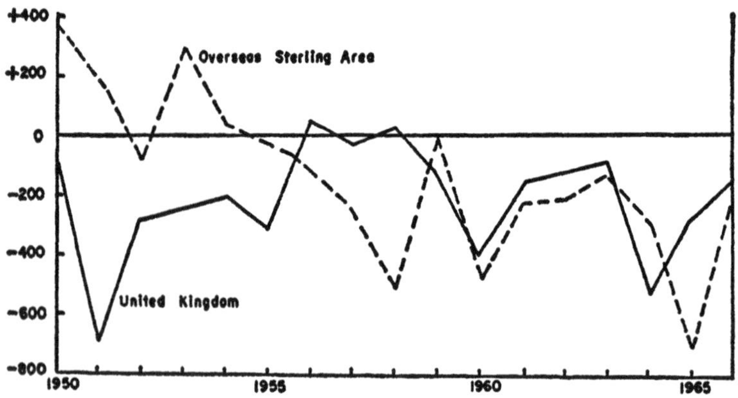

Visible Trade Balance of the U.K. and the O.S.A. 1950–66

SOURCE Cooper, op. cit., p. 185.

In the 1930s when international trade was hedged about with restrictions, the existence of a multilateral trading body such as the Sterling Area was of undoubted benefit, but since the 1950s when convertibility became general this element of advantage has also disappeared. It seems very difficult to dispute the current assessment that by the end of the period membership of the Sterling Area was of only slight benefit to the British economy.

On the other hand the existence of these very large sterling holdings has undoubtedly increased the possibility of, and certainly the fear of, disruptive speculative pressures. With such a high ratio of liabilities to reserves, sterling becomes vulnerable to protective action by sterling holders whenever a deficit occurs which is regarded as being greater than 'normal' and 'acceptable' (however ill-defined the terms), or when any event occurs to create the fear of devaluation. This defence response takes the form of lagging sterling payments or liquidating holdings. The sheer size of the overseas sterling holdings makes the pressure very great when it does occur. Given the official policy of maintaining the sterling balances and/or failing to reduce them, economic policy must, to an undesirable extent, be directed to produce an external situation which induces the maintenance of these holdings. This can be done by increasing the financial reward for keeping sterling or by creating a healthy balance.

There is, of course, always a trade-off between holding sterling assets which pay interest and holding gold which does not. Under conditions of complete certainty there would be no incentive to hold gold. A threat of devaluation, however, implies the possibility of a large capital loss against the certainty of a small return. The greater the danger of devaluation, the greater the attraction of holding gold and thus the greater the reward that must be offered to induce the continued holding of sterling. Throughout the post-war period the persistent pressures on sterling have required the offer of correspondingly and increasingly high rewards. Thus interest rates have been gradually pushed up with deflationary effects on the economy.

> 'What does seem clear is that interest rates have been higher than they would have been in the absence of large sterling balances. . . . Balances that might have gone elsewhere for security were left in London because the yield was too attractive to give up. The resulting high interest rates in the United Kingdom inhibited investment and weakened the effect of government tax incentives and subsidies to stimulate domestic investment.'[8]

[8] Cooper, op. cit., p. 187.

Bond rates increased from 3·8 per cent in the first half of the 1950s to 4·7 per cent in the second half of the 1950s and to over 6 per cent in the 1960s. High interest rates not only reduce the incentive to invest but also have an immediate adverse impact on the balance of payments in that they lead to outpayments on overseas liabilities.

Despite the high return on sterling, confidence in the pound was not high and the fear of devaluation often led to periodic waves of speculative selling. Thus the second strand of policy had to be activated, of reducing the payments deficit. As has been observed, the deficits were usually the result of high growth and full employment putting pressure on the productive capacity of the economy, this conjunction occurring for instance in 1947, 1955, 1957, 1961, 1964 and 1967. The attempts to reduce the payments deficit on these occasions inevitably resulted in a reduction in the rate of growth and an increase in unemployment leading to the notorious stop-go cycle. However, since little was done to increase the productive capacity of the economy to meet potential demand, the problem was only shelved and was bound to reappear when the economy was stimulated again. There was clearly a conflict between a high and stable rate of growth and the maintenance of equilibrium in the balance of payments as long as the authorities remained determined to maintain the sterling exchange rate at a fixed parity of $2·8.

Meanwhile Britain made every effort to build up confidence in the pound. The Basle Agreement gave sterling holders a guarantee in return for the maintenance of holdings. Reserves were increased, until by 1970 they were over £1,000m. and were still being increased. This sum is far greater than the current account deficit in any one year, but Britain's position as a leading world banker at a time when confidence in the pound was not high necessitated large holdings. (In the heyday of the Gold Standard when confidence in the pound was absolute, Britain managed her international commitments with a gold backing of only £50m.) In times of deficit Britain could not afford to sell gold but instead had to borrow from other countries and from the I.M.F. who, of course, tended to impose more stringent deflationary conditions to protect their loans. On the other hand gold is essentially unproductive, and there is an opportunity cost involved in terms of the utilization of real resources when it comes to evaluating the worthwhileness of adding to reserves. By the end of the decade the position was eased somewhat by the creation of swap facilities with other countries and Special Drawing Rights at the I.M.F.

If, as seems probable, most of the periodic current account

deficits were the result of excess demand, a number of alternatives were open to the government. It could have devalued the pound, but the maintenance of parity was an article of faith with all governments and only under the most dire circumstances as in November 1967 were governments prepared to reduce the value of the pound. (In June 1972 the government did unpeg the pound from its fixed parity and allowed it to float with surprising ease. This may indicate a fundamental change in government priorities, but of course is outside the scope of this study.).

The government could have aimed at a long-term growth rate compatible with the long-term growth of productive capacity and international commitments. This would mean explicitly accepting a target growth rate lower than would be politically acceptable. It could have been possible to increase growth potential, but this was obviously a long-term solution.

It could also have been possible to reduce international commitments to a level compatible with Britain's economic position. In the event none of these courses was undertaken so that by the end of the period the problems were still unresolved.

ADDITIONAL READING

CENTRAL STATISTICAL OFFICE *The U.K. Balance of Payments* (1971)

W. CLARKE *The City in the World Economy* (1965)

A. R. CONAN *The Problem of Sterling* (1966)

R. HARROD 'The Role of Sterling' (*District Bank Review*, December 1966)

L. C. HUNTER AND D. J. ROBERTSON *The British Balance of Payments* (Edinburgh 1966)

A. KRASSOWSKI 'Aid and the British Balance of Payments' (*Moorgate and Wall Street*, Spring 1965)

L. YEAGER *The International Monetary System* (New York 1965)

CHAPTER 8

The State and Economic Growth

The Inter-war Period

Almost without exception, governments in advanced industrial countries have come to exercise, during the twentieth century, a steadily increasing influence on the growth of their economies. This influence is applied through a variety of policies, whose connection with growth may be direct or indirect, conscious or unconscious. In theory, indeed, any decision of government which alters the availability or allocation of resources may be said to have an effect on the rate of growth. Thus even nineteenth-century governments in Britain played some part in economic development, by interesting themselves, for example, in commercial relations with other countries, in the education and training of the labour force, and the maintenance of a stable currency. More deliberately, since 1914, the state has come to concern itself with such matters as the rate of investment, technical innovation, the distribution of income and wealth and the aggregate level of demand.

Although it is true to say, therefore, that economic growth as such did not become an explicit aim of government policy in Britain until (at the earliest) 1945, long before then decisions of state had made a considerable impact on the development of the economy. It is thus both possible and necessary to analyse the importance of policy measures throughout the whole period since 1918. Moreover, even if the governments of the inter-war years lacked a conscious preoccupation with growth, they already clearly admitted a responsibility for the broader, more ill-defined subject of 'welfare'. In practice this meant that whilst they continued to be inhibited in their activities by a prevailing economic orthodoxy which was hostile to state intervention, nevertheless they were confronted by certain social problems like mass unemployment which they felt an obligation to alleviate. The failures and omissions of the politicians of that generation to remedy unemployment are not termed so merely from hindsight. And it is obvious enough that had those governments devised policies adequate to deal with their acknowledged responsibilities, they would thereby have changed the rate of economic growth.

Furthermore, the powers and resources enjoyed by the governments of 1918–39 were so considerable that their behaviour was bound to have widespread economic repercussions. They had monetary and fiscal authority far beyond that of the Victorian or Edwardian state. Public expenditure as a proportion of national income rose from 15 per cent before 1914 to around 30 per cent in the 1920s. Investment by local and central government and public utilities accounted for half the gross domestic capital formation in the early 1930s. In addition, the coalition administration of 1918 inherited (even if it did not long retain) elaborate economic controls created during the First World War; and the state kept certain powers to intervene in the management of ostensibly private institutions: for instance, the Bank of England, the railways, and public utilities.

The sphere of government economic activity had thus been much expanded since the pre-war years. Of its various additional sources of power, the most important was probably that conferred by the increase of its revenues and expenditures. Two areas of new public spending especially deserve to be singled out. The sums devoted to transfer payments in the form of social security benefits rose rapidly with the advent of near-universal unemployment insurance in 1920 and of contributory old-age pensions in 1925. Although the relief given to the old and unemployed was not generous, and only slightly redistributive as between high and low income groups, it did serve to help maintain the level of consumer demand during the depression period. The amount of unemployment assistance varied less than might have been predicted from the frequent amendments to insurance legislation, since normally local expenditure on poor relief varied inversely with national disbursements. Even more effective as a contra-cyclical device, however, was state expenditure on goods and services, and capital investment. Here various administrative and political departures in the 1920s had a significant impact on the level of activity. The amount spent on road building (by both central and local government) increased from £20½m. in 1920 to £65½m. in 1930. Housebuilding was another novel form of government enterprise in which both national and local authorities took part. Of houses built between 1919 and 1939, rather more than a quarter were provided by councils and about one-third were subsidized by the state. Finally, the expenditure on rearmament rose rapidly from about 1935, appropriating 37·6 per cent of all public expenditure by 1938.

The motives which prompted these new expenditures were, however, political rather than economic. There was little or no attempt, that is to say, to use public finance as an instrument of economic management. Housebuilding was undertaken by the government because of the desperate shortage revealed by the First World War and the disorganization of the industry. Unemployment insurance was designed initially to appease the radicalism of organized labour after the war, and became accepted during the depression as the most convenient means of preventing widespread destitution. Rearmament was obviously a military imperative, which Chamberlain as Chancellor supported only with reluctance. Even road building, the measure most deliberately conceived to alleviate depression, was intended to rehabilitate the unemployed or to ease the financial problems of distressed local authorities, rather than to reduce unemployment *in general*. In consequence, the actual influence of government spending on the condition of the economy was less than it might have been, particularly since expenditure was cut and not increased during years of crisis like 1921 and 1931. Only the rearmament programme of the 1930s was immune to such setbacks – and hence probably operated more successfully as a stabilizing factor, in the recession of 1937–8, than any previous kind of government expenditure.[1]

If we examine fiscal and monetary *policy* in the 1920s – as distinct from those measures which raised government expenditure without any special regard to their effect on the economy in general – we find that its objects were modest and its outcome discouraging. From the end of the war the principal long-term goal of monetary policy was the restoration of the Gold Standard, formally abandoned in March 1919. Bankers, politicians, and many economists felt that the Gold Standard system had brought such benefits to Britain in the past, that its resuscitation was imperative. And though it was admitted, in some measure, that a return would involve some economic disadvantages, these were assumed to be temporary and tolerable.

The other principal object of financial policy was the reduction of the national debt. This had increased some fourteen-fold since 1914 (at least a quarter of the cost of the war had been met by loans) and by the late 1920s its servicing claimed 46 per cent of the annual budget. But whilst the reduction of the debt appeared desirable to both Labour and Conservative governments, the adoption of this

[1] This is not to say that government expenditure had no contra-cyclical effect in the earlier slumps of 1921 and 1931. Though spending was reduced on each occasion, it fell only slowly, especially in real terms.

priority entailed taking a blinkered view of other problems. Balanced budgets, even budget surpluses, became indispensable for debt redemption. Interest rates were regarded from the point of view of their impact upon conversion operations, rather than their effects on industrial activity. And though the diminution of the debt meant eventually the freeing of resources for other uses, in the short term it may well have involved the transfer of resources from those with a higher propensity to consume (taxpayers) to those with a higher propensity to save (bondholders). From all points of view debt redemption inclined the governments of the 1920s and early 1930s towards deflationary, or at least non-expansionary, policies.

The reduction of unemployment, in contrast, was not regarded as a major object of policy until the latter half of the decade (though it played a part, among other considerations, in Baldwin's abortive tariff reform proposals in the 1923 election). Prior to about 1927, heavy unemployment was regarded as the product of cyclical fluctuations, of special post-war problems of European currency stabilization, and of industrial unrest. When the abnormal and peculiarly British features of the problem were accepted, besides, solutions were sought within the confines of those monetary and budgetary policies that had already been initiated.

Even within these limits it was possible for the state to take certain constructive measures: to increase its expenditure, whether on public works or unemployment relief, by raising taxation or by borrowing. The notion of a contra-cyclical public works policy had been recommended as early as 1909, by the Minority Report of the Poor Law Commission, and had aroused some interest in the current Liberal government.[2] After 1920, however, administrations of all colours were equally reluctant to adopt such courses, holding that inflation would ensue, that business confidence would be damaged, and that state enterprise would prove administratively objectionable. The Treasury further advanced the argument, which apparently held sway from about 1924 to 1930, that increased investment by the government must necessarily be at the expense of private investment, and could increase the aggregate of employment only if it were more efficient. Though this view was absurd in the prevailing circumstances of large-scale unemployment, it evidently convinced both Snowden and Churchill during their respective chancellorships.

Rejecting the 'inflationary' remedies for depression, the government were left with deflationary ones. Unemployment might be

[2] The Alden Committee was appointed in 1913 to inquire into the application of such a policy.

attributed, not unconvincingly, to the fall in British exports (by £228m. in current values between 1919 and 1930).[3] Barring devaluation, a revival of exports was thought to require lower costs at home. This might mean two things: industrial 'rationalization' aimed primarily at maximizing economies of scale in production; and lower wages. Both answers were consistent with classical, marginalist theory; and both found support, at least in an abstract way, amongst professional economists during the 1920s.[4]

These cures for unemployment were, however, open to decisive practical objections. Rationalization and amalgamation in industry might in theory increase sales (at home and abroad) in the long run, but their advocates were forced to acknowledge that their short-term effects would include further unemployment. Though enlightened employers and moderate trade unionists could agree on the advantages at a time of cyclical prosperity – as they did in the 'Mond–Turner' talks of 1928 – neither was so enthusiastic (nor leaders as representative of their rank and file) during the downswing of the economy which followed.[5] In any case there was comparatively little which the *government* could do to further rationalization, unless it took powers to coerce or brigade industrialists. In the 1920s, at least, it was reluctant to embrace such methods.

As for wage reductions, few economists or politicians felt that this was a realistic answer to depression. It is true that the labour movement harboured dark suspicions about the government's intentions, especially in 1926 and 1931. But although most Conservative ministers probably felt that wage cuts were desirable, they – and especially Baldwin – were never willing to pay the cost of widespread industrial warfare to obtain them. The General Strike itself was, for the government, a constitutional and not an economic question. In other disputes, ministers intervened as conciliators, not *agents-provocateurs*. Following the end of the General Strike, the Prime Minister himself appealed for reconciliation, and his wishes were respected at least so far as the preservation of conditions of work were concerned. Nor were those cuts in public salaries imposed in the 1931 crisis paralleled by any widespread attack on wages in the

[3] See above, pp. 108–12.

[4] E.g. W. H. Beveridge *Unemployment: A Problem of Industry* (1930 edn), pp. 359–72, 416–20, and *Causes and Cures of Unemployment* (1931); T. E. Gregory, 'Rationalization and Technological Unemployment' (*Economic Journal*, vol. 40, 1930); H. Clay *The Post-War Unemployment Problem* (1929).

[5] Contrast the T.U.C. *Report*, 1929, pp. 199–200 with the evidence of Arthur Pugh to the Macmillan Committee in 1930 (Mins. of Evid. Qs. 4619–23) and Bevin's speech at the Labour Party Conference 1930 (*Report*, pp. 197–8).

private sector. There was at no time in this period any indication of a conspiracy to lower wages, nor any possibility that a policy could be conceived on this basis.

The only government measure specifically intended to assist exports – apart from minor credit facilities and some tax reductions in the 1920s – was the Gold Standard itself. When the Treasury and the Bank of England argued and manœuvred the return to gold in 1926, they expected a world-wide stabilization of exchanges, the end of inflation and depreciation and the resurgence of business confidence to provide the basis for a revival of world trade. Since the assessment of foreign expectations, the role of confidence and the powers of example were so important to the decision, the authorities were equally dogmatic about the symbolic necessity that the new rate of exchange should be the same as the old: $4·86 to the pound.

Their insistence was notoriously mistaken. Keynes estimated that the chosen rate of return overvalued the pound by about 10 per cent, and although this figure was disputed at the time, and remains dubious, the point that there was *some* overvaluation seems indisputable. In addition, the expectations which Lord Norman rested on this demonstration of good faith by Britain were mostly unjustified in the aftermath. Other countries, notably France, showed no hesitation in undervaluing their currencies. Gold was frequently hoarded rather than released into the world monetary system. Prices continued to be partially 'managed' by governments, including that of the U.S.A., in accordance with domestic interests. There was no significant move to return to free trade. In these conditions, British exporters were obviously handicapped, not helped, by the decision of 1925. The basic industries were immediately affected by a further loss of competitiveness abroad. And it seems likely that the state of the exchanges also hindered the expanding industries in gaining a foothold in world markets during the later 1920s. The disadvantages persisted until Britain went off gold in 1931; and thereafter conditions in the international economy were less helpful than before to the recovery of British exports.[6]

[6] The point is sometimes made that since the Gold Standard lasted only six and a half years its effect on British overseas trade must have been relatively unimportant. Two considerations weigh against this view. Firstly, the period 1925–9 was the only one of marked expansion in the world economy during the whole inter-war period (except for 1919–20). Secondly, there is a causal relationship, even if not a perfectly watertight one, between the overvaluation of 1925, the devaluation of 1931, and the collapse of the world trading system thereafter. Britain's economic recovery in the 1930s was slower in part because of the repercussions which her abandonment of gold had on other nations.

The domestic consequences of the return to gold were less pronounced than the external effects. Keynes had argued that restoration must involve deflation and higher unemployment, if the balance of payments and gold reserves were to be protected.[7] In the event, Norman and the Bank seem to have made a fairly conscious effort to prevent the fulfilment of these prophecies: keeping bank rate down until the very eve of the 1931 crisis, and allowing the commercial banks a relatively free hand in dispensing credit. One of the consequences of this policy was probably the rapid increase in foreign lending in the late 1920s.[8] The other was that the gold reserves were never, in fact, secured against speculation. Indeed, the Bank necessarily came to rely on attracting short-term capital funds in order to offset its lack of gold, so that by 1928 Britain had acquired net, short-term, capital liabilities of £300m. The Gold Standard was thus critically vulnerable to unexpected capital movements, which might equally be caused by the existence of profit-making opportunities abroad (as in 1928/9); by the need of foreign financiers for liquidity (as in July 1931); or by fears of devaluation by Britain (as in August and September of that year). Whilst industry at home did not suffer to any great extent from the monetary policy of the Bank after 1925, therefore, it was, ironically, to pay the price of the Bank's undue lenience, in the draconian deflation and commercial crisis which accompanied the financial emergency of 1931.

The year 1931 marked a turning point in policy, but less so, unfortunately, in the thinking behind policy. The Gold Standard was abandoned (albeit involuntarily) for a controlled exchange system. Free trade gave way to protection and imperial preference. A monetary policy influenced largely by external factors was superseded by a policy of 'cheap money' geared to purely domestic requirements. Yet whilst these departures might have formed the basis of a more radical and interventionist approach to the unemployment problem, in the event the governments of the 1930s did not follow them up. Fiscal policy changed scarcely at all. Industrial and regional policy was only slightly modified. Thus the impact of what changes there were in the conduct of economic affairs was greatly reduced. And recovery, even by 1939, was far from complete.

The continued conservatism of the government in budgetary matters was amply demonstrated in the depression years of 1931–3. The initial swingeing economies of September 1931, affecting unemployment benefits, public works, teachers' salaries and the rest,

[7] J. M. Keynes *Economic Consequences of Mr Churchill* (1926).

[8] See above, p. 133.

were perhaps justified in part as an attempt to maintain the Gold Standard and (after its abandonment) to prevent a catastrophic decline in the parity of sterling.[9] Even so, the National Government exceeded its prescribed duty of balancing the budget, by enforcing similar cuts in local authority spending, and thus accentuating the degree of deflation. In addition, it refrained from any step towards restoring these cuts and lowering taxation until 1934, when the worst of the slump was over. For the rest of the decade, too, successive chancellors refused to alter their stands of opposition to any policy of public works or deficit financing to remedy unemployment. They adhered to this attitude now, moreover, when the external consequences of such policies were much less alarming, when economic opinion was much more favourable, and when other countries were engaged in proving their practicality.

The potential advantages to be gained from unbalancing the budget (or even from increasing government expenditure via taxation) were thus ignored during the 1930s.[10] This may in part have reflected the government's satisfaction with the rate of economic recovery, and its (certainly exaggerated) faith in the efficacy of the measures that had been taken. Probably, too, conservatism was still implanted in the departments of the civil service – not only the Treasury, but also those ministries responsible for spending on public works and social services. But perhaps most important was the consideration of confidence, which always weighed heavily with those in charge of financial policy. It seems that the government and its advisers continued to feel that a bolder policy would be upsetting to domestic and international investors. But the latter had ceased to be a significant factor now that the free flow of capital and trade was so much a thing of the past; and in fact the government itself maintained at least a partial ban on foreign lending throughout the decade. As for industrialists at home, there was no direct evidence to show how they would react to a more ambitious state policy. In any case it was evidence that their 'confidence' was insufficient to allow more than a very slow increase in capital formation in many sectors of the economy. Their mood was determined, naturally enough, largely by the low marginal efficiency of capital, which balanced budgets did nothing to improve.

The National Government thus rested most of its hopes on cheap

[9] See H. D. Henderson, 'The Economy Report', in *The Inter-War Years and Other Papers* for the importance attributed to confidence by one who opposed the economy measures on economic grounds.

[10] See Tables 51 and 53, pp. 172–3.

money. Bank rate was lowered to 2 per cent by 1932, and stayed there until 1951. Credit was plentiful, and new credit institutions were established to fill those gaps in the network of agencies for industrial lending which had been noticed by the Macmillan Committee in 1931.[11] But the economic effect of this monetary policy (something of a misnomer) is difficult to assess. For some developing industries it was probably a boon. Simply because of their comparative newness, firms in such industries were more likely to come to the market for finance than older undertakings, having had little opportunity to build up their own reserves. There is some evidence, accordingly, that the revival of the issue market in 1932–3 was most marked in the motor car and other consumer goods industries. The scale of these industries was still too small, however, for it to be possible to talk of a *general* revival of investment or borrowing until two or three years later. In most spheres of production returns on capital were simply insufficient in the early 1930s for any investment, however low its cost, to seem justified.

The chief beneficiary of cheap money was not thought to be manufacturing, however, but house building. In this case, though there is some uncertainty about the importance of low interest rates in initiating the boom of the 1930s, their part in encouraging and prolonging it is fairly well established. The housing industry employed some 6 per cent of all insured workers in these years, and attracted a net investment of £140m. in 1934, so that its contribution to the recovery of the economy as a whole, allowing for the effect of the multiplier, was considerable. It might have been larger still, had local authority enterprise and government subsidies continued at the level achieved in the 1920s, instead of being allowed to fall off.

In so far as the governments of the 1930s exercised a direct influence upon industry (as distinct from providing indirect financial stimulants to investment and expansion), their object appeared to be the reduction of competition. Here, as with tariff protection, the politicians of the 1930s seemed to be breaking with the assumptions of a perfect, free market economy, upon which most contemporary economic theory still rested. It was not coincidental, presumably, that their boldest innovations occurred in those spheres where business interests were most likely to make larger profits as a result.

Rationalization took a number of forms. One common variant was that of market-sharing agreements, through which individual firms restricted both output and sales. Under the Coal Mines Act of

[11] Macmillan Report on Finance and Industry (Cmd. 3897, 1931); H. Clay *Lord Norman* (1957), pp. 351–3.

1930, for example, a scheme of this kind was administered by district syndicates, which were later strengthened by legislation imposing fines on delinquent members. Similar arrangements were made, with the backing of the government or of the Bankers' Industrial Development Company, in other industries such as cotton and shipbuilding, where the price-fixing machinery was supplemented by schemes for the destruction of excess capacity.

The rationale of cartelization was that the reduction of competition maintained profits and investment, which otherwise would fall catastrophically. Whether this was so in fact, it is impossible to say.[12] Rationalization projects did tend to keep inefficient firms in being, especially in the coal industry, but this might well have been consistent, under conditions of depression, with preserving employment and output. Though the policy of curtailing production and capacity in basic industries certainly reduced the labour force, continued liberalism and rivalry could quite easily have reduced it more, especially in the areas that were already worst affected.

Rationalization could scarcely pose as a regional policy, however, and manifestly failed to offset the government's failures in this sphere. The large disparities in regional unemployment rates during the inter-war years have already been considered.[13] No serious attempt was made by the government to grapple with the problem of concentrated unemployment until the late 1920s, and no policy was ever devised in this period whose authority or scale corresponded to the difficulties. The government did substantially reduce local rates on industrial firms in 1928. But this measure served only to lessen the disincentives to industrial activity in the depressed areas, not to create any incentives to move to them. The main concern of the state in the years after 1928 was, in fact, to transfer excess labour out of such regions. Not until 1934, with the passage of the Special Areas (Development and Improvement) Act, was a more positive attitude to regional policy adopted. Commissioners were appointed for each of the home countries, with the task of persuading industrial enterprises to shift to these euphemistically designated blackspots: South Wales, south-west Scotland, Tyneside and north Durham, and west Cumberland. They were allowed to offer certain inducements, including, by the end of the decade, tax concessions. A limited number of trading estates were built for lease, with government funds. But such measures as these, designed to attract industry to the

[12] For some discussion of the point, see A. J. Youngson *Britain's Economic Growth 1920–66* (1967), p. 100.

[13] See above, p. 37.

depressed areas, were adopted only during the last two years of the peace; only, that is, after the previous hopes of a spontaneous movement of firms had proved futile. In all, no more than about £5m. was spent on industrial grants by the Commissioners for England and Wales. And at no stage was the policy shifted from a voluntary to a compulsory basis. Industrialists (except foreign refugees) remained free to build on sites in the south and Midlands. Thus of nearly 4,000 factories opened in Great Britain in 1932–8 only 139 were situated in the Special Areas, less than 4 per cent of the total – whereas well over 40 per cent were in Greater London.

The impression left by a study of government policy in the twenty years after 1918 is of an enduring attachment to conservative habits of mind. All governments, Coalition, Conservative and Labour, inhabited a world shaped, intellectually, by 'long-dead theorists'; they upheld balanced budgets and sound finance, abhorred inflation and bureaucracy. The most deeply felt party controversy over economic policy concerned the much-overrated issue of tariffs, which proved when adopted to have only marginal effect for good or ill.[14] The most radical change of policy, arguably, was the abandonment of the Gold Standard, which no party wanted and all tried to avoid.

On the other hand, the politicians of this era were not entirely impervious to fresh ideas. Their fault was perhaps less that of sheer inflexibility than of lack of confidence and conviction, rendering them unwilling to carry out radical experiments except on a scale so modest as to be self-defeating. They appeared, like many British conservatives before them, as reluctant and tentative agents of change, which might have been more rapid had they chosen to resist it *à outrance*. Thus small programmes of public works were financed throughout the depression, except for brief lapses in 1925–6 and 1931–4, without ever occupying more than 12,000 to 15,000 men. A cheap money policy was followed during the 1930s, unaccompanied by any fiscal incentives to investment; and a regional policy was introduced with good intentions but without teeth. Rationalization was helped and encouraged, but not, except in rare instances, enforced. Public expenditures on welfare and housing remained at unprecedentedly high levels, but obvious gaps in the welfare state were left unfilled (family allowance, a health service), and existing expenditure was pruned during times of stringency. In short, the career of inter-war governments was replete with opportunities for fruitful intervention in economic life, but almost all of them were wasted. The state did, largely by accident, help to alleviate the full

[14] See above, p. 115.

impact of the depression. But though it provided ballast for the economy, it gave little motive power.

Economic Policy since 1940

The Second World War, although in some respects a less visible break with the past than the first had been, was none the less the origin of a series of economic and social transformations. In the context of economic policy the earliest, and perhaps the most important, development was the arrival of Keynesian ideas, with Keynes himself, at the Treasury. The budget of 1941 was the first testimony to his influence, using taxation to regulate aggregate demand, and estimating the size of the wartime 'inflationary gap' from officially compiled national income data. Keynes' thinking was just as apparent in the preparations made for the reconversion of the economy to peacetime conditions. Beveridge's publication of *Full Employment in a Free Society* in 1944 was particularly important in this respect, for advocating the use of government expenditure and taxation as economic stabilizers, though still placing secondary reliance on manpower controls and powers over industrial location.[15] The government itself had already been committed to accepting full employment as an objective following the White Paper on this subject earlier in the year, even if the proposals of this document were less far-reaching than were Beveridge's. The obligation was sufficiently strong, and the means to fulfilling it sufficiently tried, to ensure that the policy changes required would be made, whatever political party came to power.

During the war, too, the scope for government economic intervention, whether on Keynesian or more orthodox collectivist lines, was greatly enlarged, firstly by the increase of public taxation and expenditure, secondly by the rapid creation and extension of a variety of physical controls. In 1939–45, as in 1914–18, the conception of what was an acceptable level of taxation changed permanently. Thus total government expenditure at constant prices rose from 26 per cent of G.N.P. in 1933 to 30 per cent in 1938 (helped by rearmament) and to almost 40 per cent by 1950.[16] An average of 34 per cent of personal income was taken in taxes by 1950, as compared with 20 per cent in 1938. The controls that were imposed, soon after war began, affected prices, labour mobility and the allocation

[15] Keynes himself was however less optimistic than Beveridge about reducing unemployment to a maximum of 3 per cent; see Beveridge's prologue to the 1960 edition of *Full Employment in a Free Society*.

[16] See Table 53, p. 173.

of all important industrial materials, although the government did not assume direct responsibility for industrial production in more than a minimum of cases. And the external difficulties arising from the decline in British exports and almost total economic dependence on the U.S.A. for credit during the war guaranteed that these concessions to bureaucracy would not be quickly retrieved.

Finally, the war was followed by the election of the first majority Labour government, with an ideological posture and an administrative disposition different from any inter-war government (including those of 1924 and 1929–31). The difference was due less to socialist doctrines, however, than to the political and social impact of heavy unemployment in the 1930s and six years of total war. Many of the policies nurtured by the new government, such as the Beveridge plan, had been hatched under the Churchill coalition; and many of its promises were electoral commonplaces.

The economic problems of the post-war period were different from, but no less complex than, those of the previous generation. The burden of mass unemployment was removed. But the demands of war had created vast external debts and deficits. Moreover, the very ambitiousness of recent governments has made life more difficult, by multiplying the goals to be pursued. This diversity of objectives has become the hallmark of economic policy since 1945. The state has set out to attain, usually in conjunction, not just full employment but price stability, a positive balance of payments, security for sterling, a fairer distribution of income (variously defined), larger expenditure on public services and, finally, economic growth. The management of the economy has entailed an attempt, constantly taxing, to reconcile these diverse aims.

Of the various governmental concerns here noted, the maintenance of a favourable balance of payments has probably been the most persistent and influential. There is no doubt that this problem took precedence in the minds of the post-war Labour administration over the achievement of maximum economic growth, and even over more cherished ideals of equality and the socialization of industry. The preservation of physical controls, fiscal policy, and the attempt to operate an incomes policy, were alike conditioned by this central preoccupation.

Physical and fiscal controls were partly interchangeable. Labour, though it referred from time to time (as in the 1947 *Economic Survey*) to the conception of a planned economy, employed its direct powers over supply and consumption chiefly to restrict domestic demand and to make scarce materials available for export industries. Such powers became redundant, therefore, as scarcity grew less acute and as fiscal measures proved to be a more simple and flexible check on consumption. The Labour government itself relinquished most of the wartime controls it had inherited, between 1948 and 1950. And Dalton and Cripps began the process which was to convert the Treasury into perhaps the most sophisticated budgetary machine in the developed world. Until the outbreak of the Korean War, the Labour government was well set on a course of restoring 'free enterprise' in most sectors of the economy, and of substituting the policy ideas of Keynes for those of the Webbs and the National Joint Council.

The only new control sought by the government in the later 1940s was applied to wage increases. Between 1948 and 1950 Cripps, as chancellor, tried with some success to hold down pay rises and dividends. He did so, however, purely by moral suasion, securing the voluntary co-operation of the T.U.C. General Council. And since the exercise of restraint was demanded as an emergency measure, and in fact came to an end in 1950, it could scarcely be regarded as part of an established economic policy. Its acceptance in the short term owed much, probably, to the personal authority of Cripps himself.

The other measures which lent distinction to the Labour regime were, of course, the nationalization of transport, coal and power, and steel. The economic repercussions of this legislation are, however, more difficult to assess than the political. The industries brought under public ownership were given little time to adjust to their new status before the government fell; the first long-term development plan for the coal industry, for instance, was not published until 1950. In addition, public investment projects were seriously affected by the continued financial stringency of these years.

Already under the Labour government, however, the nationalized industries were victims of uncertain and ambiguous policies. Perhaps the major justification for state appropriation – certainly in the case of coal and steel – was the need for internal reorganization in these industries, which had been hampered in the past by private vested interests. But once nationalization had been put through the fundamental question arose of whether public enterprises should operate primarily as suppliers of cheap services or materials to other industries, or should observe ordinary commercial principles. More recently, perhaps, the choice might be expressed as one between taking decisions by reference to their social rather than their private costs. The first policy is liable to waste resources, or at least to create deficits. In the early years of the National Coal Board, for example, prices were averaged as between efficient and inefficient pits, and profitable and unprofitable markets. A wholly commercial line of policy, however, serves to conjure up the spectre of irresponsible and inhuman monopolies. The Labour government, at least, showed no sign of solving this dilemma. Their doubts, and those of their successors in the 1950s, were apt to be translated into arbitrary and irregular ministerial intervention in the affairs of the public enterprises, especially in the sphere of pricing policy and investment.

Judged in relation to its more immediate objectives, however, the economic policies of the Labour government enjoyed perceptible though inconsistent success. The primary aim of correcting the post-war balance of payments deficit was largely realized by 1950, though further progress was interrupted by the effects of the Korean War. In addition, the government had carried out an ambitious welfare programme, and had maintained a more equitable distribution of scarce goods and services than any peacetime predecessor (though it did not, thereby, do much to equalize incomes). Unemployment had been kept at a low level, except during the 1947 fuel crisis, though it has been persuasively argued that the government deserved little direct credit for this.[17] On the other hand the external stability of the economy was never fully secure. The country arrived at comparative solvency only by way of a convertibility crisis in 1947 and a substantial devaluation in 1949. The problem of inflation was never solved, and was bound to have grown more serious around 1950, even without international conflagration, as the result of the end of wage restraint and the continued pressure of high public expenditure. In the last analysis, however, the reconstruction of a peacetime economy had been accomplished remarkably quickly since 1945; and if the Labour government had worried little about prices and sterling its electorate probably felt that it had been quite austere enough.

From a longer perspective the economic management of the Labour administration is seen to have introduced a regime of Keynesian fiscal policy which was to be adhered to (with some variation and supplementation) by all subsequent governments. The first duty of the state had come to be regarded as the balancing of supply and demand, the preservation of macro-economic equilibrium embodying full employment and external balance. How reliable and effective was the application of this policy to be?

[17] R. C. O. Matthews, 'Why Has Britain had Full Employment Since the War' (*Economical Journal*, vol. 78, 1968).

The most immediate problem of fiscal management is that of acquiring information. The object of stabilization requires an assessment of the state and fluctuation of demand, which governments have found difficulty in making promptly and accurately. For want of other data they have relied heavily, until recently, on unemployment statistics; but these were sometimes an unreliable indication of the level of demand, and almost always a belated one, subject to a lag of around twelve months. Thus corrective policy measures have customarily followed in the wake of changes in the pressure of demand rather than anticipating them: at best reducing the effect of the remedies, at worst transforming them into a disturbing element exaggerating the cycle they were intended to cure.

The operation of such a budgetary policy creates further difficulties. Most forms of government expenditure, whether capital investment or transfer payments, were not easily subjected to short-run variations. Either they represented contractual obligations or they were essential to efficiency and planning in the public sector. As has been noticed, when nationalized industries, for instance, were starved of investment in economic emergencies they performed worse than they might have done for considerable periods thereafter. In these circumstances, the main burden of adjustment fell upon taxation. But taxes were liable to political constraints; it was easier to lower than to raise them, and easier to alter indirect or corporate taxes than direct. There was no increase in personal direct taxation at all between 1951 and 1966. Thus the whole task of fiscal management came to depend predominantly on the manipulation of a miniscule number of controls – which, predictably, often proved insufficient for the purpose.

The main instrument of fiscal regulation apart from purchase taxes was company taxation. This, too, however, has been an unsuitable means of counteracting economic fluctuations. When initial allowances on investment were introduced in 1945 their purpose was obviously to encourage higher capital formation. This objective has been maintained in the changeover to investment allowances in 1954 (widening the tax exemptions allowed to company investment) and to investment grants in 1964 (replacing exemption by cash refunds). But all these devices designed to increase investment were exposed to revisions and cuts according to the needs of the current economic situation. Their value as incentives was therefore obviously lessened. Unfortunately, not much was gained in efficiency of fiscal management. Alterations of company taxes took longer to work their way through the economic system than almost any other changes in taxation. The lag preceding corrective government measures to deal with a particular cycle was thus followed by a further lag (of up to nine months) preceding their impact.[18] The outcome was to make it even more likely that fluctuations would be accentuated rather than prevented.

The Conservatives, coming to power in 1951, were not unaware of the shortcomings of fiscal techniques of control. They were determined, however, as soon as the international situation permitted, to liquidate the surviving wartime restraints on the economy, most of which had disappeared by 1954. They also somewhat reduced the direct economic authority of the state, by denationalizing the steel and road haulage industries. To make up their hand, as it were, they had recourse to controls in the monetary sphere, employing and extending with great energy mechanisms which had lain unused for twenty years.

Monetary policy in the 1950s comprised a number of different devices. The most familiar was the bank rate, which was altered twenty-four times between November 1951 and October 1964. These changes were, however, frequently no more than advertisements of the government's general view of the economic situation. At most their real usefulness was probably limited, and recognized to be limited, to the external sector, where changes in the rates of interest could influence the movement of short-term capital.

Adjustments of the bank rate were supplemented by other, more refined methods of influencing credit. The government developed the practice of relaying official 'requests' to the commercial banks concerning their loan-making policy. And in 1958 they introduced a special deposits scheme by which the banks could be required on order to lodge a stipulated proportion of their liquid assets with the Bank of England. Both powers were intended to restrain demand, though the former was capable of more discriminating applications: to favour exports, for instance, above domestic consumption. But neither was of more than secondary importance in the monetary arsenal as a whole.

On the domestic front, the chief method of monetary control was government variation of hire purchase regulations. This power was considerable but clumsy. Hire purchase was used almost exclusively for the sale of consumer durables, which accounted for only 8 per cent of total consumer expenditure and 5 per cent of final sales. Thus adjustments in the conditions governing credit facilities had to be

[18] J. C. R. Dow, 'Fiscal Policy and Monetary Policy as Instruments of Economic Control' (*Westminster Bank Review*, May 1960. Also August and December).

pronounced in order to have effect; and the strain to which a narrow range of commodities were subjected probably damaged their long-term prospects of growth and profitability.

By the end of the 1950s, the reliance on such monetary instruments for the purpose of stabilization was coming under increasing criticism. In the first place, the force of impact of such regulators was questionable. Probably only hire purchase controls had an immediate and guaranteed effect on demand. The government's trust in its own policy had obviously been at times excessive. Before the 1955 election, for example, the Conservatives tried to rest the whole burden of holding back excess demand on action in the monetary sphere, whilst indulging in a mildly expansionary budget. The result was a sudden emergence of external pressure, which necessitated a much more stringent budget in the autumn.

Secondly, the accurate timing of monetary initiatives was not much easier than that of fiscal measures. The former had the advantage of not being tied to a parliamentary budget. But the problem of estimating current economic trends remained the same. The government customarily regarded the level of foreign currency reserves as their main indicator of the need for monetary curbs; but this, like unemployment, was usually a fairly late symptom of changing economic conditions. Thus the Treasury's exercises in equilibration by monetary and other means, in 1952, 1955, 1957 and 1960, invariably looked like emergency responses to full-grown crises, the more so because restrictions were apt to be introduced *en bloc*.

Following the third of these crises, when Mr Thorneycroft was defeated in his attempt to impose a rigid limit on the supply of money, opinion inside and outside the government swung against the purist monetary policy that had ruled hitherto. The change of attitude was helped by the influential public criticism of past policy, both monetary and fiscal, by the Radcliffe Committee on the Working of the Monetary System in 1959, and the Plowden Committee on Public Expenditure in 1960. At this point the Conservatives began looking for alternative economic instruments of a more experimental kind – accepting thereby the need both for more selective measures to deal with particular problems, and for a larger degree of state intervention in economic life.

The years between 1958 and 1961, indeed, represented something of a crisis of confidence in British public life. Not only the government itself, but many other interested organizations and professional commentators felt the insufficiency of Britain's economic performance during the 1950s. Though the failure of policy had not been by any means complete – average unemployment remained low, and the standard of living improved consistently – there were at least three sources of major dissatisfaction. Firstly, inflation remained a constant problem; prices had risen throughout the decade far more than any chancellor had thought desirable. This tendency was clearly linked with the persistent insecurity of Britain's external position which is discussed elsewhere.[19] Secondly, although the nation as a whole had enjoyed increasing prosperity and full employment in these years, the incidence of these benefits had not been evenly spread. The existence of under-privileged areas in the north and west recalled the circumstances of the 1930s. Finally, and most important, the rate of growth of the British economy was found to compare unfavourably with that of most Western European countries. The irregularity of growth experienced in Britain at different times in the 1950s itself indicated the difference between potential and performance here. Other countries seemed to have avoided that unevenness of expansion, and thus to have achieved or be about to achieve higher living standards. It was widely held that the government should regard a higher growth rate as an explicit and supreme objective, and one by which its activities in other particulars should be regulated.

The example of Western Europe taught no single or necessary lesson. It was possible to argue from foreign experience, both that a more liberal policy should be adopted, aiming at greater competitiveness in a freer market; or that a more *étatiste* approach, emphasizing planning, should be taken. Social, political, and possibly temperamental factors inclined the government, at this stage, in the latter direction: towards the French model of indicative planning. The lead tentatively given by the Conservatives in their 1959 term was followed more enthusiastically by the Labour administration which came to power in 1964.

A variety of initiatives were launched in the third post-war Conservative administration which together represented at any rate a partial conversion to planning. All of them took as a starting point the aim of an improved and consistent rate of growth. This priority was most evident in the establishment of the National Economic Development Council in 1961. The N.E.D.C. published two major reports early in its life: *The Growth of the U.K. Economy to 1966* in March 1963, and *Conditions Favourable to Faster Growth* a month later. They were intended as an 'examination of the economic

[19] See above, Chap. 7, and for inflation in general, F. Paish *Studies in an Inflationary Economy* (1962).

prospects of the country stretching five years or more into the future';[20] and represented the product of co-operation between representatives of employers, trade unions and government. The first and more predictive report on growth was not without merit as a feasibility study, involving investigation of the development plans of seventeen individual industries. But the rate of growth it proposed, 4 per cent per annum, assumed among other things the winning of a substantial balance of payments surplus by 1966, which in the event proved far too optimistic.

As an answer to the parallel problem of inflation, some at least of the members of the N.E.D.C. were in favour of an effort to introduce an incomes policy. This idea, however, received no such general support as the broad object of growth. Conservative efforts in this direction were vitiated by the government's apparent subscription to a 'demand–pull' theory of inflation, which incidentally saw higher unemployment as a possible remedy for price increases. Such a view was supported by some, though not all, of the economic literature of the time.[21] The trade unions for their part refused to participate either on the Council on Prices, Productivity and Incomes in 1957, or on its successor, the National Incomes Commission, in 1962. The idea of an incomes policy was further discredited by Selwyn Lloyd's fiat, imposing a 'pay pause' on public employees, in July 1961. Here, as in the field of regional policy, the Conservatives failed to convince the sceptics of their good intentions.

Many Labour innovations after 1964, however, followed upon earlier developments, and carried further towards realization the idea of indicative planning. The foundation of the N.E.D.C. and the reorganization of the Treasury carried out in 1962 facilitated the creation of the new Department of Economic Affairs, which incorporated sections of both. Incomes policy progressed a crucial stage further, with the acceptance by the unions of the National Board for Prices and Incomes. The machinery of regional policy was also greatly elaborated; and the Ministry of Technology took over the existing Department of Science, the Ministry of Aviation and the National Research and Development Corporation.

These initiatives culminated in the publication of *The National Plan* in September 1965, when what the popular journalists succinctly

[20] Selwyn Lloyd, quoted in E. E. Hagen and Stephanie White *Great Britain: Quiet Revolution in Planning* (Syracuse 1966), p. 25.

[21] For which see B. McCormick and E. Owen Smith (eds) *The Labour Market* (Part 8), and A. W. Phillips, 'The Relation Between Unemployment and the Rate of Change of Money Wage Rates' (*Economica* 1958).

called 'growthmanship' reached its zenith. This document set out its purposes, briefly:[22]

> The projections in the Plan are essentially attempts by Government and industry, working in co-operation, to break down the general objectives of a 25 per cent growth rate [over the next five years] into the implications for particular industries.
>
> These projections should help firms and industries to take more informed decisions than if they were left in the dark about other people's intentions and beliefs.

The emphasis on voluntaryism, planning by bark rather than bite, is evident. The *sine qua non* of such an approach, however, is accurate and convincing forecasting. In the event, the Plan was abandoned within a year, when stringent deflationary measures were taken to meet the sterling crisis of July 1966. And the primary cause of its failure was certainly the adoption of an excessive growth target which the authors were ill-prepared to vary. The proposed rate was, it is true, later scaled down to 3·8 per cent per annum, to take account mainly of revised estimates of the labour supply. But in view of this revision, the rate of growth of productivity envisaged by *The National Plan* was higher than that previously proposed by the N.E.D.C. This could not be achieved without a rise in investment and demand in excess of anything justified by the British balance of payments situation. Reliance on increased output and productivity to solve this problem was simply a miscalculated risk. After this first attempt, moreover, the idea of planning suffered eclipse. A revised edition was discussed in government circles, but postponed ostensibly on the ground that application to join the E.E.C. by Britain made future prognostication difficult. All that was produced, eventually, was the shorter 'planning document', *The Task Ahead*, in February 1969.

The other main plank of the Labour government's economic policy was control of prices and incomes. In theory this had a sound basis, as it became clear that price rises could not be fully prevented by dealing with excess demand through established budgetary methods.[23] In practice, however, the Prices and Incomes Board encountered growing difficulties, especially in its relations with the unions. Though it managed to enforce a wages standstill from July 1966 to January 1967, thereafter it appeared able to delay pay

[22] *The National Plan* (Cmnd. 2764, 1965), p. 3.

[23] For later discussion of the problem of prices in relation to incomes, see W. Fellner *et al. The Problem of Rising Prices* (O.E.C.D. 1961), and N.I.E.R., 'Wage Rates, Earnings and Wage Drift', vol. 46, 1968.

increases but not to diminish them. It led, rather, to a greater aggressiveness on the part of the unions, so that at one point the Labour administration seriously contemplated legislation intended to restrict their strike activity.[24]

This recent political commitment to promote a faster rate of growth in the economy through increased state intervention has clearly not been rewarded by any great measure of success. Even before the Conservatives were returned to power in 1970, Labour had dismantled some of its planning structures: the Department of Economic Affairs disappeared in 1969, and the government published its intention of merging the Prices and Incomes Board with the Monopolies Commission. To say what went wrong with this policy experiment, however, is still a hazardous undertaking. It is obvious that for the state to involve itself more intimately in economic affairs poses its own problems for government. One such problem would appear to be simply that of raising unduly high expectations of immediate results. The hopes pinned on the National Plan, for instance, were no doubt exaggerated, partly because of the spurious precision of the predictions it made. Their disappointment seems to have been a sufficient deterrent to the continuance of this kind of experiment. The aura of the national incomes policy was similarly transient, for it was never likely that this would achieve increased productivity, a reduction in inflation and a more equitable distribution of wages at one and the same time. And this observation points to a further, intractable problem. The more multifarious are the activities of the state, the more policy conflicts will tend to appear. It is easy to point to signs of inconsistency in the conduct of recent governments: in trying to tackle the problem of unemployment in the regions, for instance, whilst raising overhead labour costs by the imposition of S.E.T., redundancy benefits and higher insurance payments; or in opposing the Ministry of Technology and the Industrial Reorganisation Commission (both inclined to encourage private amalgamations) with a stronger Monopolies Commission. There is no necessary contradiction between measures such as these; but the probability of collisions increases the more policy vehicles the

[24] In the White Paper *In Place of Strife* (Cmnd. 3888, 1969). For the administration of the incomes policy, and its general effectiveness, see H. A. Clegg *System of Industrial Relations* (1970), pp. 418–40, and *How to Run an Incomes Policy and Why we Made Such a Mess of the Last One* (1971); H. A. Turner, 'Collective Bargaining and the Eclipse of Incomes Policy: Retrospect, Prospect and Possibilities' (*Brit. Journ. of Indust. Relats.* 8, 1970); F. Blackaby and M. Artis, 'On Incomes Policy' (*District Bank Review* 165, March 1968); R. G. Lipsey and J. M. Parkin, 'Incomes Policy: a Reappraisal' (*Economica* 37, 1970).

government puts on the road. And the destination to which the traffic in general is being directed cannot always be clearly seen.

Has the phase of enhanced government economic activity since the late 1950s brought any benefits? Some achievements can be listed which, though not monumental, are at least useful and durable. Firstly, the economic expertise brought to bear on policy decisions has undoubtedly increased. The training given to civil servants has become more rigorous, and more professional economists and statisticians have been attached to the Treasury and other departments. Largely as a result of this influx, many aspects of government accounting, planning and forecasting have become more efficient and sophisticated in character. The publication of the White Paper on *The Financial and Economic Objectives of the Nationalized Industries* in 1961 and of the first five-year departmental expenditure programme in 1963 are cases in point. Finally, there has been marked progress in the field of industrial research and development in this period, to which the official patronage of government departments such as the Ministry of Technology has contributed.

None of these advances brings the solution to the problems of democratic economic management much nearer. But the short answer to those who blame the government for the whole of Britain's recent economic deficiencies is that the state, for all its tendency to encroach and expand, is neither autocratic nor prophetic. To expect the government to enjoy unqualified success in ameliorating the condition of the economy is as chimerical as it is, say, to expect a police force to abolish crime.

TABLE 51

Government Expenditure 1900–55

	At 1900 prices (£m.)	At current prices
1900	£280·8	280·8
1920	565·3	1,592·1
1938	851·2	1,587·0
1950	1,195·0	4,539·0
1955	1,309·0	6,143·0

SOURCE Peacock and Wiseman, table 2.

TABLE 52

Current Expenditure of Central and Local Government, 1955–68

	Central	Local
1955	5,102	1,096
1960	6,813	1,715
1965	10,156	3,152
1968	14,192	4,383

SOURCE *Annual Abstracts of Statistics, 1961 and 1969.*

TABLE 53

Government Expenditure on Selected Items

Percentage of G.N.P. at current prices

	Nat. debt	Defence	Social services	Econ. and environmental services
1900	1·0	6·9	2·6	2·5
1920	5·4	8·6	6·8	3·7
1938	4·0	8·9	11·3	3·9
1950	4·4	7·2	18·0	5·7
1955	4·2	9·6	16·3	4·3
1968	6·1	7·9	24·1	13·0

SOURCES Peacock and Wiseman, table 9; *National Income 1969.*

ADDITIONAL READING

D. H. ALDCROFT *The British Economy: The Interwar Years, 1918–39* (1970)
R. BAILEY *Managing the British Economy* (1968)
E. M. BURNS *British Unemployment Programmes, 1920–38* (Washington 1939)
R. CAVES *Britain's Economic Prospects* (Washington 1968)
S. R. DENNISON *The Location of Industry and the Depressed Areas* (1939)
J. C. R. DOW *The Management of the British Economy, 1945–60* (Cambridge 1965)
J. AND A. M. HACKETT *The British Economy* (1967)
K. HANCOCK 'Unemployment as a Problem of Public Policy, 1920–39' (*Econ. Hist. Rev.* 16, 1962–3)
U. HICKS *The Finance of British Government, 1920–36* (1938)
N. KALDOR 'Conflicts in National Economic Objectives' (*Economic Journal*, vol. 81, 1971)
G. MCCRONE *Regional Policy in Britain* (1969)
D. E. MOGGRIDGE *The Return to Gold, 1925* (Cambridge 1969)
E. NEVIN *The Mechanism of Cheap Money* (1955)
S. POLLARD *The Gold Standard and Employment Policies between the Wars* (1970)
P.E.P. *Economic Planning and Policies: Britain, France and Germany* (1968)
G. L. REID AND K. ALLEN *Nationalized Industries* (1970)
H. RICHARDSON *Economic Recovery in Britain, 1932–39* (1967)
E. A. G. ROBINSON *Economic Planning in Britain: Some Lessons* (Cambridge 1967)
B. E. V. SABINE *British Budgets in Peace and War, 1932–45* (1970)

R. S. SAYERS *Financial Policy 1939–45* (1956)
SIR R. SHONE 'Planning for Economic Growth in a Mixed Economy' (*Economic Journal*, vol. 75, 1965)
R. SKIDELSKY *Politicians and the Slump* (1970 edn)
B. TAYLOR 'The N.E.D.C. after Six Years' (*Westminster Bank Review*, February 1968)
R. TURVEY *Public Enterprise* (1968)
D. WILLIAMS 'Montagu Norman and Banking Policy in the 1920s' (*Yorks. Bull.* 11, 1959)
D. WINCH *Economics and Policy* (1970)
G. D. N. WORSWICK AND P. ADY *The British Economy 1945–51* (Oxford 1952); *The British Economy in the 1950s* (Oxford 1962)

CHAPTER 9

Conclusion

The reader has been warned, from time to time in earlier chapters, not to expect clear-cut resolutions to this discussion of the history of economic growth. The purpose of this conclusion is therefore not to offer bold judgements but rather to excuse timid indecision. And the principal justification for timidity must, of course, be the difficulty of showing proof or gaining acceptance for any single explanation of the pace and pattern of economic expansion since 1918.

Firstly, however, it should be pointed out that economists disagree not just about their explanation of economic growth, but also about its desirability. On the one hand, for example, Dr Mishan has written a number of polemical attacks on 'growth-mania', asserting that 'doubts about a positive connection between social welfare and the index of economic growth are amply justified'.[1] His argument rests chiefly on an analysis of the 'external diseconomies' or 'disamenities' of unregulated growth, in the shape of environmental pollution or psychological stresses. On the other hand Professor Lipton, observing the same landscape, writes that 'growth is not a quantified version of increasing happiness, but is the nearest approach to it that economics can provide'.[2] He appears to suggest that growth has fostered art as much as acquisitiveness; and that the problem of traffic congestion, say, can be solved by more underground car parks built from the increased resources it denotes.

The chosen theme of this book, however, does not imply any opinion on the merits of this controversy so far as the authors are concerned. We do not wish to say that the maximization of economic growth should be the paramount aim of the British government or people in the future. We do, however, admit to another value judgement: a belief in the importance of economic efficiency. By this we mean that the consumption of economic resources by society should be no greater than is necessary to provide properly for its wants or needs. Our criticism is thus generally directed at the failure

[1] E. J. Mishan *The Costs of Economic Growth* (1967), p. xviii.
[2] M. Lipton *Assessing Economic Performance* (1968), pp. 50–1.

to avoid wasting assets. The requirement of efficiency does not mean the maximization of growth, because though it may represent a standard for assessing our success in producing the goods and services which we choose, it does not govern the nature of that choice by linking it to the overriding goal of the highest possible aggregate production. It is not 'inefficient' for society to value and foster some activities wherein 'productivity' is necessarily low or its measurement difficult – though it may be inhibiting to growth. There remains the difficulty, of course, of deciding what balance of social activities is most desirable; and the further difficulty, that in almost all productive occupations economic and non-economic elements are mingled: efficiency and job satisfaction are not synonymous. These problems are the subject of an argument which ranges far beyond the conventional boundaries of economic science; though it is an argument, of course, in which economists can be expected to take part.

If the present book takes as a central theme economic growth rather than efficiency, therefore, this is primarily a matter of convenience. In a study of the national economy it is helpful to concentrate on a problem which has been the concern of macro-economic theory, rather than one which has been the subject mainly of marginalist analysis. In addition, it seems possible to assume that, historically speaking, economic growth and economic efficiency have been closely connected. Though individual industries may experience contracting output and rising productivity, the economy as a whole has probably never done so. Finally, the statistical record of economic growth is somewhat more complete and easily handled than the evidence relating to changes in efficiency. Whilst it may be possible to compile a satisfactory productivity index for manufacturing industry, for instance, it is much more difficult to do so for the service sector of the economy.

This is not to suggest, of course, that the explanation of past economic growth is a straightforward matter; indeed, the inconclusiveness of this inquiry must be exonerated by its complexity. The factors which might explain economic growth are numerous, and different in kind. Some of them are not strictly economic. Many are difficult to assess quantitatively. And the contribution of any single factor, even if theoretically measurable, is often difficult to separate out in practice from the complex pattern of economic cause and effect. These methodological pitfalls will become more obvious, however, if we review some of the possible elements in the growth process.

The factors affecting economic growth can, for the purposes of argument, be grouped into three broad categories, which might be labelled environmental, structural and managerial.[3] This differentiation points firstly to the contrasting *levels* of explanation for economic behaviour, and to the varying historical perspectives which can be adopted. 'Environmental' factors are those long-term social and cultural conditions which fall partly or wholly outside the normal scope of economic analysis, but which influence – perhaps crucially – the character of economic development. They have been referred to from time to time in this book, especially under the heading 'management and industrial relations'. Both entrepreneurs and workers were seen, in that chapter, to be products of a class structure which shapes their attitudes to each other and conditions their economic objectives. Consumers, likewise, tend to behave in ways which are adapted to social norms, and which may help or hinder economic growth – by their readiness, for instance, to accept mass-produced goods, their preference for buying services rather than manufactures, or their choice of leisure occupations. The role of the state in economic life is likewise the outcome of a wide variety of non-economic factors: determining the choice of policy objectives, the methods by which decisions are taken and carried out, the influence of competing interest groups, and so forth.

Clearly, therefore, a host of imponderable elements may be taken into account in discussing economic growth. The process of abstracting one aspect of social activity for study is necessarily hazardous. The social history of Britain since 1918 must have reacted significantly upon its economic history. But to assume that it did so is certainly inconvenient for the conduct of economic analysis. Most economists would argue, accordingly, that whilst social circumstances impose certain limitations on the scope of economic activity and the speed of change, these limitations are both ill-defined and constant. They prevent the overthrow of private property or the abandonment of Sunday dinners. But they do not explain *variations* in economic growth over short periods of time; nor do they account for shifts in the average growth rate as between one economic period and another.

The evidence on which these assumptions are based, however, is

[3] These terms refer to types of explanation rather than types of factor. For more elaborate classification of the factors involves, in the historical context of the first industrial revolution, see R. M. Hartwell, 'Causes of the Industrial Revolution' (*Econ. Hist. Rev.* ii ser., 18, 1965); and A. W. Coats, 'Economic Growth: The Economic and Social Historian's Dilemma' (Nottingham 1966).

unavoidably tenuous. Even economists probably do not believe that environmental factors are absolutely constant. They might well admit, for example, that if the average rate of growth of the British economy has altered markedly between the periods 1900–14, 1918–39 and 1945–68, part of this change is likely to be attributable to the social and political impact of the two world wars.

Such a possibility raises interesting problems of an interdisciplinary kind. Did the economic growth, high by international standards, enjoyed by Britain in the 1930s spring from previous or contemporaneous social change (contrasting with the political conservatism of the inter-war period)? How far have the more sharply fluctuating growth rates of some European countries since 1918 been associated with rapid social transitions? How far, in either case, can social trends be attributed to merely economic causes? These questions have, hitherto, received only slight attention.

Even if we are inclined to attribute some weight to environmental factors in economic development, therefore, we may find difficulty in assessing even the direction of their influence. It is clearly not necessary to suppose that such an influence always reinforces current economic tendencies. In Britain's case, we may be disposed to stress the fact that economic growth accelerated during the 1920s or the 1940s. Or we may be struck instead by the modesty of such movements in the growth rate; indeed, in no twenty-year period since 1873 has the speed of expansion departed more than about one percentage point from the average for the whole of that period. This stability suggests that the long-term effect of environmental factors has been inhibiting to growth. And it would not doubt be easy to find circumstantial evidence for strong and continuous conservative forces in British society which might support this thesis. If the evidence remains conflicting, the moral is not that it should be ignored, however, but that it has been too readily neglected in the past. Economists have considered social change where it can be easily quantified (as in the case of demographic trends) but otherwise overlooked it. Economics as a discipline has suffered by sacrificing its social content to its scientific methods.

The 'structural' explanation of British economic performance is similar to the environmental in its emphasis on long-term factors, but restricts itself to specifically economic variables. By far the most common structural theory is that outlined in Chapter 1, concerning the intrinsic characteristics of mature economies. The 'maturity' thesis has many versions, however, and in its more recent formulations is certainly more sophisticated than it was in the work of Schumpeter or Hoffman. In particular, as was suggested in Chapter 1, it is now conceived as an account of the constraints on increases of economic capacity rather than of the determinants of recorded growth rates.

The original application of this structural argument to British economic history led to consideration of the disadvantages of an 'early start' as an industrial nation. This circumstance was held responsible for shaping an economy highly dependent on a number of staple export industries using relatively simple techniques and increasingly vulnerable to foreign emulation. There can be little doubt that the basic pattern of British industrial production and overseas trade had become a handicap by the late nineteenth century, and remained so (though to a diminishing extent) during the inter-war period. The alteration of this pattern was necessarily a slow process, inasmuch as the previous commitment had been large.

The maturity thesis has been lately adapted, in addition, to explain the unsatisfactory performance of the British economy since the Second World War. It has been held that those countries which experienced slow growth over the depression period, suffered most economic destruction during the war and recovered from it later, have since displayed superior powers of growth – part real, part illusory – as a result.[4] Britain was less well endowed in recent years with opportunities for replacing plant and reapplying resources. Furthermore, her ability to achieve rapid increases in productivity was the more limited because the backward sectors of her economy had previously dwindled into insignificance and because the labour supply was inelastic. And in the peculiarly situated economy of the U.K. the relative prices of labour and real investment have been credited with the major responsibility for technical and productivity change. Finally, it is possible to argue that the rate of improvement of national productivity is largely an outcome of the growth of output in the manufacturing sector, and that those countries like Britain which had already established a high volume of output in manufactures and were more inclined to divert available resources into expanding their services grew more slowly as a result.

The structuralist explanation of growth (and retardation) has the attraction of conferring a certain immutability upon the shape of the past. It should be pointed out, however, that this thesis is less long-term than might appear. Different attributes of maturity have

[4] J. Knapp and K. Lomax, 'Britain's Growth Performance: the Enigma of the 1950s' (*Lloyds Bank Review*, October 1964).

been fixed upon at different times to account for economic sluggishness: the overcommitment to slow-growing industries in the years from the late 1870s to the late 1920s; the low rate of return on investment in the 1930s; the lack of underutilized resources and labour since 1945. None of these factors retains its importance for longer than a generation or two. It might be suggested, on this evidence, that structural defects in the economy tend to be self-correcting over time (and the rising unemployment rate since 1965 might perhaps indicate that the recent phase of labour shortage is passing). Certainly it is clear that maturity does not prevent a long-term acceleration of growth, or *a fortiori* of potential growth, such as has occurred in Britain since 1900/14. Whilst these observations do not disprove the maturity thesis, they do render it somewhat more diffuse.

What is more, none of the assertions made about the structural capabilities of the British economy have gone unquestioned. They have, on the contrary, been characterized as pessimistic in mood and unprovable in fact. The favourite cudgel of their critics has been the comparison of British growth rates (especially since 1945) with those of other economies showing some or all the features of maturity credited with hampering expansion. It can be argued, also, that the British economy has itself proved capable of achieving rates of growth well above its norm, albeit only in short and erratic bursts, and that no long-term explanation of growth patterns has adequately accounted for these irregularities.

Without attempting to arbitrate in this controversy, it can legitimately be considered whether many of the attacks on the structuralist school do not reflect different economic perspectives rather than differences of analysis. The maturity thesis may well arouse misgivings mainly because it appears to discount the importance of economic policy – management – as an influence on economic growth. But it is quite consistent to hold that although structural factors have assumed more significance than policy in a historical context, they need not continue to do so. In most respects the structuralist analysis derives from an examination of Britain's past economic performance in which the influence of policy was nugatory or served merely to reinforce pre-existing trends. The opposing managerial analysis, in contrast, reflects a primary concern with future prospects, with the possible consequences of *changes* in policy, and with the apparent success of different approaches to management in other countries.

Mr Beckerman has observed that 'almost any conceivable cause of economic growth could equally well be an effect'.[5] This proposition, apparently depressing from the point of view of economic analysis, is yet a source of optimism to those whose main concern is the management of the economy. Firstly, it implicitly denies the premise that long-term factors in economic development must always be regarded as more important than short-term ones. The secret of faster growth may be found in places quite accessible to political decision-making – for example, in adjustments of the exchange rate. The crucial achievement becomes that of initiating a higher rate of expansion. Growth is seen as a chain reaction, a cumulative process which must come to involve all elements of the economic system, and even such environmental factors as social structure and attitudes. In terms of future prospects, it is unnecessary to be preoccupied by the differences between chickens and eggs.

There remain, however, genuine differences between the structural and managerial exponents which it is important to resolve. Whilst the utility of an appropriate choice of policy may be acknowledged by the former as much as the latter, the problem of defining the objects of policy continues unsettled. One approach calls for attention to immediate economic difficulties: the balance of payments, the rate of capital formation, the inflation of prices. The other emphasizes the need to look for long-term shifts in labour and resources, an increase in specialization, and possibly an effort to change established patterns of economic behaviour.

Empirical research on such large issues is still at an elementary stage. When analysing the operation of a national economy it is not possible, except in rare instances, to take smaller units of study, individual industries or firms, as analogues. But the interpretation of global statistics is subject to numerous difficulties and ambiguities. For the layman, perhaps, there is comfort to be drawn from the observation made at the outset: that economic growth is not in itself a good; and that more time might reasonably be given to discussing the direction of our economic efforts. For the economist there can only be the consolation of knowing that the questions are intriguing even if the answers remain obscure.

ADDITIONAL READING

N. KALDOR *Causes of the Slow Rate of Economic Growth of the U.K.* (Cambridge 1966)

[5] 'The Determinants of Economic Growth', in P. D. Henderson (ed.) *Economic Growth in Britain* (1966), p. 57.

A. MADDISON 'How Fast Can Britain Grow?' (*Lloyds Bank Review* 79, 1966)
D. C. PAIGE *et al.* 'Economic Growth: The Last Hundred Years (*Nat. Instit. Econ. Rev.*, 1961)
E. ROTHBARTH 'Causes of the Superior Efficiency of U.S.A. Industry as Compared with British Industry' (*Economic Journal*, vol. 56, 1946)

INDEX

INDEX

INDEX

Index

For Product Safety Concerns and Information please contact our EU
representative GPSR@taylorandfrancis.com
Taylor & Francis Verlag GmbH, Kaufingerstraße 24, 80331 München, Germany

www.ingramcontent.com/pod-product-compliance
Ingram Content Group UK Ltd.
Pitfield, Milton Keynes, MK11 3LW, UK
UKHW022110190926
475702UK00013B/1352
* 9 7 8 1 0 3 2 1 2 9 6 5 5 *